The
Piano Owner's
Guide

THE PIANO OWNER'S GUIDE

How to Buy and Care for a Piano

Revised Edition

by CARL D. SCHMECKEL

CHARLES SCRIBNER'S SONS
NEW YORK

Charles Scribner's Sons
Macmillan Publishing Company
866 Third Avenue, New York, NY 10022
Collier Macmillan Canada, Inc.

Library of Congress Cataloging-in-Publication Data

Schmeckel, Carl D
  The piano owner's guide.

  1. Piano—Construction. I. Title.
ML652.S35 1974   786.2'3   74-7362
ISBN 0-684-13872-7

Macmillan books are available at special
discounts for bulk purchases for sales
promotions, premiums, fund-raising, or
educational use. For details, contact:

Special Sales Director
Macmillan Publishing Company
866 Third Avenue
New York, NY 10022

10   9   8

Printed in the United States of America

TO MY WIFE CELIA
AND OUR THREE DAUGHTERS

Preface

Within the limited confines of a single book it is impossible to pass on to you all of the piano knowledge that I should like you to possess. But if you absorb a good portion of the information presented here, you will be able to avoid inferior piano merchandise and service, and be in a position to know what you want and how much value you should receive for your hard-earned dollars.

CARL D. SCHMECKEL

1974

Table of Contents

PART ONE
General Information

PART TWO
Purchasing a New Piano

PART THREE
Purchasing a Used Piano

PART FOUR
Piano Care and Service

List of Illustrations

The Piano Owner's Guide

PART ONE

General Information

1. THE UNIVERSAL INSTRUMENT

A volume that aspires to offer readers a comprehensive knowledge of the piano must also recognize the need for a history of the piano, however brief. It is only fitting that the inventor of the piano and others who contributed substantially to its development should receive due acknowledgment (little enough to offer to those who have given us so much).

Bartolommeo Cristofori of Italy is credited with inventing, in 1711, the first crude fixed-keyed instrument to use hammers to draw musical tones from wire strings.

During the years that followed the invention of the first piano, instrument makers added many mechanical improvements. Among the better-known contributors were Gottfried Silbermann and Stein of Germany, Sebastian Erard of France, and John Broadwood of England. Stein is credited with inventing the soft pedal, while credit for inventing the sustaining pedal is given to Broadwood. Other contributions by Silbermann and Erard were less spectacular, but equally important.

Early pianos were roughly rectangular in shape and were

constructed in a horizontal plane, but they were without the benefit of an iron frame or plate to offer rigidity. These pianos were exceedingly unstable and required constant tuning to keep them in playable condition.

Then, in 1790, an American named John Hawkins built the first upright piano. Along with other worthwhile contributions to piano technology, he introduced a crude iron frame to increase tuning stability. Variations of this iron frame were quickly adopted by other builders (some of whom not only capitalized on Hawkins' original idea, but also tried to claim credit for it).

Until 1840, grand pianos were built almost exclusively in Europe. Then Jonas Chickering built the first American grand piano. The 20th century found the United States manufacturing and selling more pianos of every type than any other nation on earth.

The piano is recognized as the one supreme instrument in our modern musical culture. It has become the basic instrument used in the teaching of music. It is an orchestra at our fingertips, the delight of composer and artist alike. It has no peer. The piano is truly the universal instrument.

2. POPULARITY OF THE PIANO

More people are playing more pianos today than ever before in history. Piano sales in the United States have climbed over 500 percent during the past four decades. According to the National Piano Manufacturers Association, there are now almost 10 million pianos in our nation's homes. An additional half million are in our schools, churches, music studios, and entertainment spots. (Some authoritative estimates are considerably higher.)

American production is approximately 200,000 new units each year, a small portion of which is exported to other countries. Roughly 40,000 old pianos are discarded annually, which means that our overall total climbs at the rate of about 160,000 American-made pianos a year. This total does not include a steadily mounting volume of foreign imports.

The current cultural rise in the United States is reflected in an increase of more than 2 million nonprofessional pianists during the past decade. The American Music Conference estimates that there are now well over 21 million nonprofessional pianists in the country. There are also more than 5 million American children taking lessons on the piano.

3. AVAILABILITY

There are hundreds of modern American and foreign piano makes on the market. Each maker manufactures the various types of pianos in a wide range of styles. There are pianos for the home and for concert halls, and specially designed pianos for schools and churches, small apartments, and trailers.

There are miniature 64-note spinets that retail for less than $400, and there are magnificent concert grands that retail for $8,000 or more. There are pianos in all sizes, colors, and finishes, in an endless variety of price ranges.

Pierce Piano Atlas (a reference volume for the piano industry) lists the brand names of approximately 7,500 different makes of pianos, new or used, still in existence in the world today.

Manufacturers and retailers extol the virtues of their products, each claiming to offer the buyer something special in quality or price. The uninformed (or misinformed) piano buyer, faced with almost unlimited choice of product, is completely at the mercy of those who sell pianos.

It need not be so for you.

4. WHAT SIZE PIANO FOR YOU?

Your choice of a piano will be influenced by a number of factors other than the size of the instrument. But the size, along with quality of manufacture, contributes much to the musical potential of the piano. When a piano is designed, its overall size (length for a grand and height for a vertical upright) is critical to the soundboard area and the string lengths. It is highly desirable that both the soundboard area and the string lengths be great enough to contribute toward good tone. The lengths and heights of the various types of pianos vary somewhat according to their manufacturers; but in general, they conform to the eight classifications given in the following table:

TYPE	APPROXIMATE SIZE	CHOICE
Concert grand	*8' to 9' (or more) long*	first
Medium grand	*6' to 8' long*	second
Small grand	*4'–6" to 6' long*	third
Full-size upright	*48" or more in height*	third
Studio upright	*45" in height*	fourth
Console	*41" in height*	fifth
Spinet (conventional)	*37" in height*	sixth
Spinet (64 note)	*37" in height (narrow)*	seventh

Note that both the small grand and the full-size upright are rated as a possible *third choice*. This is because both types of piano have approximately the same soundboard area and string lengths. We might say that they are equal in tone potential derived from these factors.

Also note that although the conventional spinet and the 64-note (miniature) spinet generally agree in height, the 64-note instrument is considerably narrower (as little as 42

6

inches in width), which results in less soundboard area and shorter strings.

If you must purchase a small piano, it is strongly recommended that you settle for nothing smaller than *console size with a direct-blow action.* (See Fig. 4, p. 28).

Definitions

A *grand* piano, in the correct sense of the term, is a piano that is constructed on a *horizontal plane,* with strings stretched horizontally across the piano plate and framework. Only about 5 percent of pianos manufactured are grand pianos.

A *vertical* piano is a piano that is constructed on a *vertical plane,* with strings stretched vertically across the piano plate and framework. (For an illustration of a vertical piano plate and closely related parts, see Fig. 3, p. 17).

An *upright* piano is a vertical piano of any size. But in America the term is usually interpreted to mean a *very large vertical piano,* ranging from studio or school size up to sixty inches in height.

Can an upright piano be a grand piano? Not really. But occasionally we find old uprights that bear brand names followed by the word "grand." The term apparently was used by some manufacturers of the past to stimulate sales of extra-large uprights. Use of the term for uprights was misleading and unethical in the strictest sense. There are some abuses in this area today (drop-action spinets that are named consoles, for instance).

5. THE PIANO CASE

A well-constructed piano case is invariably built from the best materials. The wood is not a solid thickness. It is veneered stock (not to be confused with plywood). Veneered stock is much stronger than a single thickness of wood. It is manufactured with a soft-wood base or foundation, and covered with two or more strong layers of veneer (harder woods such as oak, maple, walnut, and mahogany). The grains of the hardwood veneers run in different directions to ensure against splits or checks in the case wood. A piano built of such materials is to be much preferred. It is strong and durable.

All piano cases are not made of the veneered woods mentioned above. In some instances certain parts of the case will be made of veneered woods and other, cheaper materials used in making other parts of the case. You will also find different thicknesses of veneered woods (used for the same purpose) in higher- and lower-priced pianos. Some of the substitutes used for good veneered woods in piano cases are ordinary plywoods, hardboard, compressed sawdust, and plastics.

The quality of the finish on a piano case is important. Just because they all shine, doesn't mean that they are all alike. There is tremendous variation. Don't be impressed if you are told that the finish is hand-rubbed. Even one coat of cheap plastic finish can be hand-rubbed. Here is where manufacturing costs are cut to the bone on some makes and models of cheap pianos.

A finishing schedule of stain, filler, one or more coats of sanding sealer, and three or more coats of high-quality varnish or lacquer, with careful hand-rubbing between coats and rubbing and polishing of the top coat, will make an acceptable piano finish. This should be a minimum. Some of the top-quality manufacturers apply a great many more coats of finish to their pianos.

One should not be misled by talk of substitute finishing materials. High-grade varnish and lacquer are still the best finishing materials for pianos. They cost more, but they are worth it.

A sketch of a *grand piano case* with the names of its parts is shown in Fig. 5, p. 33. The case parts of a *vertical piano* are shown in Fig. 1, p. 10. Familiarity with names of case parts will give you added confidence when you start that shopping tour.

6. THE "BIG THREE" AND
THE INSTRUMENT INSIDE THE CASE

The instrument inside the case consists primarily of *three* main units:

1. The structural unit.
2. The tone unit.
3. The mechanical unit.

Each of the above "big three" units consists of three other highly interrelated assemblies:

The structural unit includes (1) the piano back (2) the metal plate and (3) the tuning-pin block (wrest plank) (See Figs. 2 and 3, pp. 14 and 17).

The tone unit is composed of (1) the soundboard assembly (2) the piano strings and (3) the hammer heads (See Figs. 3 and 4, pp. 17 and 28).

The mechanical unit consists of (1) the keyboard assembly (2) the hammer-action assembly and (3) the damper-action assembly (See Fig. 4).

This simplified explanation of piano construction is intended to acquaint the piano owner with piano construction in general terms, and in as easy a manner as is possible. To augment this study, be sure to consult the illustrations noted above.

If you have access to a piano, you might lift the top or lid and remove the bottom door (if a vertical) to expose the inner construction. Caution: Beware of the curiosity of small children when you open the case. Look but *do not touch* any of the finely regulated parts. Untrained fingers can do more

Fig. 1

TYPICAL CASE PARTS of a MODERN SPINET or CONSOLE
PIANO SHOWING LOCATION and NOMENCLATURE

1. Caster
2. Ferrule
3. Pedal rail or front rail
4. Leg
5. Bottom frame or door
6. Keybed
7. Fallboard
8. Upper frame or panel
9. Top

10. Music panel or rack
11. Music-panel hinge
12. Music desk molding
13. Arm or cheek
14. Keyslip
15. Side post
16. Side or end
17. Pedals
18. Bottom board

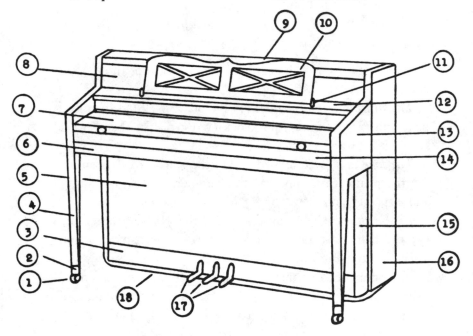

damage inside a piano in one minute than a competent piano-service man can repair in one day.

Now let us discuss each of the "big three" units in greater detail.

7. THE STRUCTURAL UNIT

A. *The piano back* is composed of a number of vertical wooden posts (usually softwoods), extending almost the full height of the piano, which are braced by other horizontal pieces top and bottom. This framework is jointed and glued together in various ways, each method aimed at attaining the greatest structural support possible from the materials used. Woods used for piano backs include pine, spruce, and ash.

B. *The metal plate* is a gray-iron casting with tremendous compressive strength that is needed to withstand the enormous overall tension of the strings. An additional desirable property of gray-iron is its damping ability (the ability to absorb vibration without movement or transference of sound, such as ringing). Gray-iron also exhibits high resistance to metal fatigue.

Gray cast-iron piano plates vary in thickness, weight, and contour design, according to the preferences of piano manufacturers. This results in varying piano-plate strengths. But in all instances the aim of the overall plate design is to achieve (in conjunction with the wooden back) the highest possible safety margin over what strength is necessary to support the string tensions. There *must* be a safety margin.

This safety factor (excess strength) can mean the difference between a stable or an unstable piano design. On the one hand, a piano will hold tension and stay in good pitch and tune; on the other, the piano will fail to stay in tune an acceptable length of time. Better built, higher-priced pianos have larger safety margins. Thus they are apt to hold their tunings better than low-priced instruments.

C. *The tuning-pin block* (wrest plank) of a vertical piano extends horizontally across the upper framing of the wooden piano back and is securely glued to the latter. The tuning-pin block, made up of several or many laminations of hard rock maple wood (laminations may vary from five to twenty or more), is about a foot wide and about two inches thick. It is used to anchor the tuning pins, which in turn anchor the strings. The upper part of the metal piano plate is screwed and bolted tightly to the pin block and the upper piano back. The remainder of the plate is screwed securely to the corner back posts and the lower bracing. Thus all three members of the structural unit become interdependent.

The grand-piano tuning-pin block (about 1¼ inch thick) is seldom glued to the wooden framing. Only very few manufacturers of the finest grand pianos still consider this procedure necessary to structural stability. Generally the grand tuning-pin block is sufficiently stable if simply screwed securely to the underside of the metal plate. This feature aids in the replacement of the block, if necessary. Stability is secured by carefully fitting the tuning-pin block against a strong metal ledge on the underside of the plate. The metal ledge anchors the pin block against the pull of the strings. The rest of the plate is screwed tightly to the wooden framework. This arrangement in the grand piano is just as interdependent for overall stability as are the three parts of the vertical structural unit.

Note: It is important for you to realize that all three members of the structural unit (piano back, metal plate, and tuning-pin block) are engineered as one unit for *combined strength*. They are so closely interrelated in regard to the combined strength that a weakness in any one of them is immediately communicated to the other two.

The chief purpose of the structural unit is to provide the piano with stability, to provide enough structural solidity to withstand the tremendous tensions applied to it by the strings. The string tension in a typical piano at American Standard A-440 cycles-per-second (cps.) pitch can easily approximate 20 tons (40,000 lbs.) of pull. This is enough to lift a double garage off its foundations!

Study Figs. 2 and 3 closely. The three members of the unit are glued and/or screwed together in a manner designed to attain maximum overall strength.

There are various methods of engineering the structural unit. Some vertical piano makers favor having the metal piano plate, in conjunction with the tuning-pin block, hold up the greater share of the string load. Thus the piano back posts need not be many in number or as thick as those of a similar-appearing piano of a different brand name. Remember this: there are some very good pianos manufactured with only two corner posts to which to bolt or screw the *extra-strong* plate. A piano of this type usually has greater weight, and some European builders favor this approach.

Most American manufacturers try to impress buyers with more and thicker posts in a piano back, which is a means of avoiding piano weight. In so doing they allot less strength to the metal piano plate and more strength to the wooden piano back. They produce a lighter piano, because they have more wood and less metal in it. Many pianos have five or more back posts in them, and piano salesmen have a field day pointing out this supposed extra strength. *But such a piano back is strong only if the manufacturer did not stint too much on the weight and strength of the metal plate.*

Contrary to popular belief, you cannot and should not judge the structural unit strength of a piano solely by the size and number of back posts it displays. The *weight* of a piano is a highly important factor in judging its structural strength. More weight points to plate strength; it indicates a heavier, stronger, metal piano plate.

So if you insist on buying a small, lightweight piano because it is easy to move around, you must be prepared to accept shorter piano life and greater upkeep costs in tuning and related services.

8. THE TONE UNIT

A. *The soundboard assembly* includes the soundboard, the curved soundboard ribs (visible from the back of the piano), the treble bridge, and the bass bridge.

The piano soundboard is positioned between the piano back and the metal plate. (See Figs. 2 and 3.) It is constructed of a number of thin boards about three-eighths inches thick glued edge to edge, and it extends from the bottom of the piano up to the tuning-pin block and across the full width of the instru-

Fig. 2

TYPICAL VERTICAL PIANO BACK   OPEN-END VIEW

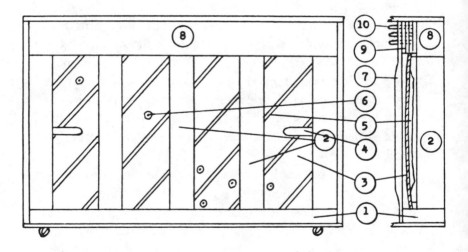

PARTS
LOCATION and NOMENCLATURE

1. Bottom beam
2. Back posts
3. Soundboard (crowned)
4. Hand dowel (grip)
5. Soundboard ribs
6. Bridge buttons
7. Cast-iron plate
8. Top beam
9. Tuning-pin block
10. Tuning pins

ment. The soundboard has a curvature (crown) on the string side, much like the top of a violin. This crown is very important to the production of good tone. A well-crowned soundboard gives life and resonance to tone, while a soundboard with little or no crown contributes to a dull, lifeless, tubby tone. Quality craftsmanship in building and fitting the soundboard in the piano has much to do with the preservation of this soundboard crown through the years of piano life. The back of the soundboard (concave side) is strengthened by a number of curved wooden ribs, and both the ends of the ribs and the outer edges of the entire sounding board are glued securely to the back framing or liner. Thus the soundboard crown is held in a state of tension, ready to respond instantly to the slightest vibration.

The woods used for soundboards must be light and elastic. Clear, straight-grained, mountain-grown spruce is considered by most authorities to be the ideal wood for this purpose. It is used in the finest pianos, generally throughout the entire piano industry. The best results are obtained when the grain of the soundboard runs parallel to the bridges and perpendicular to the ribbing.

The soundboard ribs must also be elastic. They must not hinder free vibration of the soundboard as a whole, yet they must be strong enough to withstand the pressures of the strings against the bridges and crown of the soundboard. Perfection in soundboard ribbing promotes resonance of tone and is just another of the hidden costs of fine piano manufacture that are generally unknown to the piano buying public. Conifer woods are those most used for ribbing materials.

Both the treble bridge and the bass bridge are made of hard rock maple wood, and their undersides are curved to conform with the crown of the soundboard. They are securely glued and screwed to the board. Their positions on the soundboard are also critical to good tone production. As you know, the primary function of the bridges is to transfer vibrations from the strings to the soundboard with the least amount of hindrance.

Note: Through the years many experiments have been conducted in a never-ending search for a musically acceptable piano soundboard made from materials other than wood. (Most piano manufacturers spend a great deal of money on research.) Many of these experiments have involved the use of various metals. But to the present day, all such research has failed to find a way to achieve good piano tone with anything but wood for a soundboard.

Sometimes one hears of a piano with a metal soundboard. This is not impossible, but it is highly improbable. Many of these claims have been checked, and in every instance the soundboard proved to be made of wood. Such claims usually stem from the mistaken belief that the cast-iron plate is the soundboard.

For various commercial reasons a few piano manufacturers favor soundboards made of laminated woods, including hardwoods. This type of soundboard is sometimes guaranteed against cracking or splitting. But the fact remains: in the finest pianos money can buy, the soundboards are constructed of the finest grades of spruce (as is the top of a fine violin), and they are not laminated.

B. *The piano strings* are manufactured from the finest steel available in the world today. There are about 230 strings in a typical piano: 189 plain steel treble strings, about 32 steel bass strings (weighted with a single winding of copper wire), and approximately 9 heavier bass strings (double-wound with copper wire).

There is much variation in the total number of strings on the cheaper makes of pianos. The lack of an acceptable number of strings sometimes extends all the way through the piano scale, both bass and treble sections, although in most instances such

Fig. 3

FRONT-VIEW SKETCH of VERTICAL-PIANO PLATE,
SOUNDBOARD, and CLOSELY RELATED PARTS
(The tuning-pin block is located
behind the upper part of plate.)

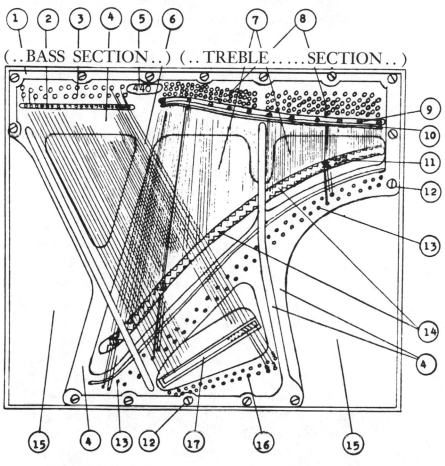

1. Piano-plate rim
2. Bass bearing bar
3. Bass tuning pins
4. Cast-iron (alloy) piano plate
5. Piano serial number
6. Bass strings (copper wound)
7. Treble strings (plain steel)
8. Treble tuning pins
9. Pressure bar (treble)
10. Treble bearing bâr
11. Bridge pins
12. Plate lag screw
13. Treble hitch pins
14. Treble bridge (maple, etc.)
15. Soundboard (spruce, etc.)
16. Bass hitch pins
17. Bass bridge (rock maple)

poor design shows up in the bass sections of pianos. (Watch for this factor when you go shopping.)

Be cautious about purchasing a piano that does not have three-string unisons (three strings to a note) in the *plain steel wire* sections of the treble area of the piano scale. There are some instances (especially among miniature spinets) where only two strings are provided for each note. These instruments (so-called) are defective. (See Item 15.)

Do not be concerned if there are two or three notes at the lower end of the treble bridge that are composed of only two *copper-wound* strings per note. (This is at the bass break, where the treble notes run down into the bass notes.) This is designed to even out and blend in the tone where the bass break occurs. It is based on good sound-engineering principles.

A few excellent makes of pianos have slightly more than 230 strings in the stringing scale. This is all to the good. Such pianos have three strings to a note in the upper bass (rather than two), and more two-string notes with fewer single-string notes in the remainder of the bass. You may find copper-wound three-string notes on *both* sides of the bass break in a top-quality instrument. This is just another indication of excellence in piano-scale designing.

A full knowledge of some of the points discussed in this section is not at all necessary to a successful and satisfactory piano *purchase*. But you may have reason to use this information as reference material sometime in the future when service work other than tuning is necessary on your piano. It is always comforting to have a grasp on a situation. For example: If a treble string should break in your vertical piano, you will realize why it may be necessary for the tuner to remove the piano action in order to repair or replace the string. Every bit of concrete knowledge you can acquire is valuable to you and to your piano.

Consult Fig. 3 to clarify for yourself the physical positions of the piano strings relative to the piano plate, bridges, tuning pins, and tuning-pin block. Fig. 3 is an illustration of a vertical piano, but practically all information contained in this section will apply to the grand piano as well.

Notice that each string on the piano is securely anchored in its position in the scale by a metal hitch pin (driven into the plate) at its lower end, and a steel tuning pin (driven through a hole in the metal plate into the wooden pin block behind the plate) at its upper end. Each bass string is looped over (around) the hitch pin, passes over the bass bridge (between two staggered bridge pins) and then up over the bass bearing bar to the tuning pin. Each wound bass string is a single length of core wire, an individual string.

In the treble section, with few exceptions, we get *two* strings (speaking lengths) for every length of plain steel wire. Each length of piano wire runs from one tuning pin, under the treble pressure bar, over the treble bearing bar, downward across the bridge, then is looped around the hitch pin, back up over the bridge, across the treble bearing bar, under the pressure bar, and up to the next tuning pin (where the wire end is anchored through a small hole in the tuning pin and coiled around same). Don't allow the terminology to throw you. Just a few minutes spent tracing the courses of the bass and treble strings in Fig. 3 will set you right.

You will notice that as you progress upward from the lowest string in the bass, the strings become shorter, note after note, until at the highest treble string the wire is only a few inches in length. Much the same thing occurs in the thickness (gauge) of the strings. The gauge of the lowest bass core-wire (and also the copper winding) is the thickest. From this point upward through the treble to the shortest steel string, the thicknesses of the strings diminish according to a set plan (stringing scale) designed for that particular style of piano.

We have already touched upon the tremendous overall

tension (about 20 tons) of the 230-odd strings when they are tuned to Standard A-440 cps. pitch. You will be reading more about this later. This overall tension is distributed throughout the stringing scale as evenly as possible by the use of differing string lengths, thicknesses, and so on.

The goal of every piano-scale design is *a well-balanced tension throughout the scale.* This balance is tremendously important, both musically and structurally. You will find better-balanced scales in the higher-priced instruments.

Now when you compare two different styles or makes of pianos, both with similar beautiful cases, you should have a better idea of why one instrument is priced at $595 and the other is priced at $995. *There is hidden quality differential.* Always buy the best that you can afford. The extra cost will profit you in the long run.

Let us examine what happens when a piano hammer strikes one of these strings that we have been discussing. Immediately upon contact the string is set to vibrating (cycling) at a predetermined rate of speed (governed by its tuned pitch). The "A" above middle C, for example, should cycle 440 times per second. At the point where the string passes over the bridge, these vibrations are communicated through the bridge to the soundboard, which immediately begins to vibrate at the same frequency as the string is vibrating. The soundboard amplifies the vibration by setting the air or atmosphere on either side of it to fluctuating at 440 cycles per second. These amplified fluctuations are called sound waves. They travel at a speed of over a thousand feet per second. Our eardrums pick up these sound waves, and we interpret them as a piano tone or note: in this case "A" above middle C. The soundboard can amplify any number of different frequences or vibrations all at the same time.

The entire tone unit: soundboard, strings, and hammer heads are closely interrelated in the production of good piano tone. Each part of the unit must do its job well. Now let us examine the part that the piano hammer heads play in this tone-producing combination.

C. *The hammer heads* are not just wood and wool felt mallets used to set the strings to vibrating. They are precisely engineered, delicately constructed, finely balanced parts that help to give "voice" and "tone color" to the piano.

If we were to install inferior-quality hammers in an otherwise excellent piano, the quality of tone would be considerably lessened. By the same token, if we equipped a low-priced piano with a set of premium quality hammers, we would certainly improve the tone. The quality and condition of the hammer heads in a piano are extremely important to the creation of good tone. In general, piano buyers and owners alike do not fully realize this.

Top-quality (premium) piano hammers (manufactured with highest-quality pure wool felt) cost more than hammers made from inferior felts. Therefore, the more you pay for your piano, the more likely you are to receive quality throughout, including piano hammers. Everyone wants a piano that is capable of producing good tone.

What is meant by a reinforced piano hammer?

At one time the term *reinforced* meant that the felt of the piano hammer head was not only glued to the hammer-head molding (core) under extremely high pressures, but the glue bond was reinforced with steel staples driven through the butt ends of the felt into the wooden molding. (See part 37, Fig. 4.)

Through the years, I have repaired many small pianos built in the 1930s, the hammers of which were peeling because the metal wire staples hadn't been used. These piano manufacturers were cutting corners in the cost of wire and labor. As a result, it is now costing their customers more money to have these pianos repaired and restored to use.

The factory blunder described above is offered by way of

demonstrating that piano-factory methods and ideas are in no way infallible. Piano manufacturers make their share of mistakes.

During the past decade, a new type of *reinforcing* has become widespread in the construction of piano hammers. This type of reinforcing entails treating the upper and lower shoulders of the hammer felt with chemical solutions to stiffen the wool fibers.

This type of reinforced piano hammer is being accredited by manufacturers and dealers alike as having desirable qualities not possessed by untreated hammers. Manufacturers claim that this new type of hammer is more shock-resistant and more resilient, improves tone, and will hold its original shape better through the years.

This is not entirely true. These treated hammers make piano tone louder and more brilliant. But as far as *improving tone* is concerned, if builders continue to promote this chemically treated hammer, they will improve good piano tone out of existence.

These treated hammers, together with widely used high-tension scaling (see Item 22), are the main reasons why modern small pianos are giving piano tuners the "harmonic fits" and are causing disappointed piano owners to ask: "What ever happened to the nice, mellow tone that pianos used to have?" or "Why do these new pianos sound so metallic and tinny?"

Present methods of chemically reinforcing piano hammer felts make the hammer felt much too hard. Hammer felt must be strong, firm, and be able to withstand many years of shock without change of shape and loss of resiliency. But the hammer felt must never be hard. Hardness destroys the deep, mellow, fundamental tone that most buyers prefer in a *home* piano. Excessive hardening of the hammer felts promotes tones abounding in partials (harmonics), which drown out the mellow fundamental tone and cause a piano to acquire a too-brilliant, metallic, or tinny sound.

Piano manufacturers know these facts. They also know that the average piano buyer is not aware of them. An uninformed public is offered a louder sound in a too-small piano, at the sacrifice of much more desirable good piano tone. There seems to be an unspoken belief throughout the piano industry that the average piano buyer does not know good piano tone when he hears it. Actually, the buyer is given little choice in the matter—when practically all of the commercial grade (low or average priced) pianos on the present market are equipped with hard, chemically treated hammer felts. Under such circumstances, the buyer has little chance to make intelligent comparisons.

We all know that the new small, compact pianos cannot deliver the same depth of tone associated with the full-size uprights when new. But there is little sense in destroying the best qualities of tone that exist in these small pianos by promoting the use of *chemically reinforced* hammers, and all for the sake of a little louder sound.

In most climates piano hammers gradually harden with use, temperature changes, and age. This hardening of the felt normally occurs over a period of years. It is an undesirable condition that should never exist at the time that the piano is retailed; nor should it occur within just a few months or a year after the piano is placed in a buyer's home.

It is highly desirable for piano manufacturers, piano service men, retailers, and others to cooperate in promoting the piano industry as a whole. But wholesome business ethics must take precedence over profit-motivated cooperation. The latter can too easily take the form of a coverup for faults and shoddy practices within the various branches of the industry. This should never be countenanced.

For an explanation of tone regulating and hammer voicing

see Item 56. Tone regulating and voicing of piano hammers in the home after purchase will not normally be paid for by either the piano retailer or the manufacturer. Present-day piano warranties do not cover this situation.

The reader should now be acquainted with many of the tone-producing properties of piano hammers, especially the new *reinforced* hammer. Hammers are very important parts of the tone unit. Do not be misled by far-fetched claims extolling the virtues of the chemically reinforced piano hammer. There is every reason *not* to prefer them, and not to pay more just because a piano has them. You could be far happier with a piano equipped with premium-quality hammer heads without chemical reinforcing.

This brings up another important question. *Can one buy pianos without chemically reinforced hammer felts?*

Many makers of very fine pianos, and a very few makers of commercial-grade pianos, still have not gone overboard on chemically treated hammers. They will be delighted to sell you a piano. Also, if you ask your piano retailer to obtain a certain brand of piano for you (on speculation) minus the chemically treated hammers, he might agree to cooperate, but you might have to convince him first. He could be as unaware of the undesirable qualities of treated hammer felts as you once were.

Moreover, the new-type reinforced hammers have become a sales-pitch item to impress uninformed piano buyers, and most manufacturers and their dealers in popular-priced pianos have hopped on the bandwagon.

In retrospect, we can be certain that there will be a great need for piano tuner-technicians skilled in the art of hammer-voicing in the years ahead.[1]

---

[1] Shortly after this item on reinforced piano hammers was written, the Research Department of the Woolen and Textile Industry of England announced the finding that chemical reinforcement of felt partially destroys the natural elasticity of the material.

9. THE MECHANICAL UNIT

A. *The keyboard assembly* is divided into two secondary sections: the key frame, and the wooden keys. (See Fig. 4.) (The keybed of the piano, located directly above the knees as one sits at the instrument, is not considered a part of the keyboard assembly. It is part of the structural framework.)

The key frame, positioned between the keyboard and the keybed, is a strong, light wooden structure that supports, aligns, and guides the keys. In a vertical piano the key frame is screwed down tightly to the keybed. In the grand piano the key frame is installed so that it will slide right or left and return to normal position through operation of the soft pedal. Two long rows of metal guide pins are driven into the key frame near its front edge. Another two rows of balance rail pins are driven into the center rail of the frame a prescribed distance from front and rear edges. These metal pins space and guide the keys, which are drilled and fitted with felt bushings to receive the protruding metal pins. Thus the keys, held in perfect alignment, are free to perform their leverlike functions in activating the piano hammer action.

The keys (standard 88-note keyboard) encompass seven octaves plus three extra notes. There are fifty-two white keys (naturals), and thirty-six black keys (sharps). Exclusive of the white key coverings and the visible portions of the sharps, the keys are usually manufactured from top-quality, straight-grained pine. Pine seems to lend itself best to this purpose. Modern plastics have almost completely replaced ivory and ebony as piano key coverings. But the manufacturers of some very fine pianos (especially grands) still use genuine ivory and ebony for coverings, and you can get them on other makes on special order for a price. Ivory and ebony are classed as prestige coverings for keys today. The new plastic coverings take and retain a fine polish, are very durable, and are practically immune to discoloration.

B. *The hammer action assembly* (Figs. 4 and 6, pp. 28 and 36) of a piano is an extremely complex and delicately regulated mechanism, consisting of thousands of small parts. Each piece of wood, metal, cloth, and felt performs a specific function. In some instances the regulating tolerances are so small that proper alignment of certain parts is accomplished by "feel." A fine piano action is a masterpiece of mechanical ingenuity.

There are two major types of piano actions used in vertical pianos: the *direct-blow action* and the *drop action*. The direct-blow action has been with us the longest. Some of its advantages over the drop action are the following:

1. It is mounted *above* the capstan ends of the keys. The keys used are considerably longer than those used in a drop-action spinet. The result of this setup is a direct, easy movement of parts (easy touch), a strong hammer blow and maximum tonal response.
2. There is less wear to parts.
3. There is less need for adjusting and regulating.
4. There is easier access for servicing, including removal and replacement of action during repair service.

The drop action is of comparatively recent origin, having had its commercial introduction in the 1930s. It was created to satisfy public demand for smaller and more compact pianos to fit into smaller houses. And as long as this demand exists, the drop-action spinet will continue to be a necessary evil: a means to an end.

The drop action is mounted behind and below the keys (which are necessarily shortened). These short keys operate the action with an upward pull rather than an upward push. Much good is sacrificed in the process, including hammer speed and tonal response. Extra hook-up parts are necessary, inclining these actions toward sluggishness, heavy touch, and excessive wear. Parts are difficult to service (cramped space) while the action remains in the piano. Removing and replacing some of these drop actions is so complicated and time-consuming that most service men charge extra when such work is necessary.

If the reader will refer to Fig. 4, he will gain further insight into the differences that exist between these two types of vertical piano actions. It should be obvious that the careful piano buyer will profit in both musical satisfaction and cost of future piano servicing if he will purchase a piano that is a console or larger and which has direct-blow action.

1. Large uprights have direct-blow actions.
2. Special vertical school pianos have direct-blow actions.
3. Studio uprights have direct-blow actions.
4. Console-size verticals have direct-blow actions (with the exception of a few models on which the manufacturers added an inch or two of height, used a drop action, and called the piano a console). If you are interested in a console piano, make certain that it has a direct-blow action.
5. Spinet pianos have drop actions (with the exception of a few existing models that have a special short ninety-degree direct-blow action to conserve space). These ninety-degree actions are quite good, the only criticism being that they are encased in a spinet-sized piano.

Note: Grand pianos use horizontal grand actions, the operations of which are considerably different from the two vertical-piano-action types. The operation of grand-piano actions in all sizes of modern grand pianos is very similar. (For more detailed information on the grand-piano action see Fig. 6.)

C. *The damper-action assembly* of a piano is a combination of finely regulated parts that mute, damp, or silence all string

Fig. 4

KEY and ACTION HEIGHT RELATIONSHIPS in FOUR MAIN TYPES of VERTICAL PIANOS

The reader should assume that all vertical pianos mounted on standard-size castors have keyboards of equal height (distance from keyboard to floor). Only that portion of a piano extending above the level of the keyboard will determine the overall height of the instrument. This composite sketch shows one size of vertical action for all four sizes of vertical pianos. In actual practice, studio, console, and spinet actions are reduced in size to further lessen piano height.

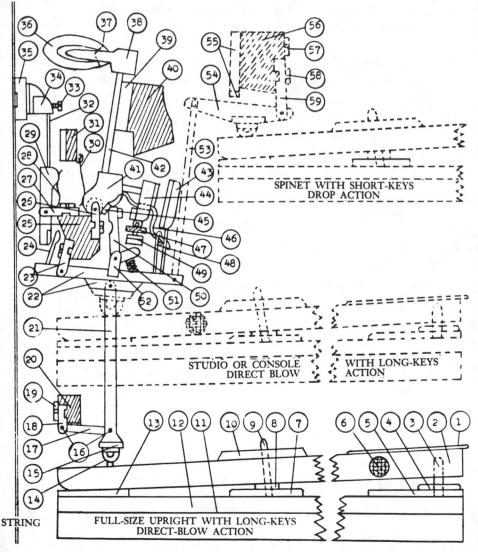

SPINET WITH SHORT-KEYS DROP ACTION

STUDIO OR CONSOLE DIRECT BLOW

WITH LONG-KEYS ACTION

STRING

FULL-SIZE UPRIGHT WITH LONG-KEYS DIRECT-BLOW ACTION

Piano parts nomenclature has never been standardized in its entirety, and we do have variations from the nomenclature listed here. But this list is typical and entirely acceptable. The piano owner should acquaint himself with the terms used.

1. Key covering	31. Hammer-spring rail (felted)
2. Piano key	32. Damper wire
3. Front guide pin	33. Damper-block screw
4. Front rail punchings	34. Damper block and head
5. Front rail	35. Damper felt
6. Key lead (weight)	36. Hammer-head felt
7. Balance rail	37. Wire staple (reinforcing)
8. Balance rail punchings	38. Hammer molding
9. Balance rail pin	39. Hammer-rail felt
10. Key button	40. Hammer rail
11. Keybed	41. Hammer butt
12. Key frame	42. Hammer stem
13. Backrail felt	43. Back check
14. Capstan screw	44. Back catch
15. Lifter or sticker felt	45. Hammer-butt felt
16. Center pins	46. Bridle strap or tape
17. Sticker guide	47. Regulating rail
18. Sticker-guide flange	48. Bridle wire
19. Flange screw	49. Regulating button and screw
20. Extension rail	50. Jack
21. Lifter or sticker	51. Jack spring
22. Wippen or rocker	52. Jack flange
23. Wippen flange	53. Inverted lifter or stocker
24. Damper-lever spoon	(drop actions only)
25. Center rail	54. Auxiliary wippen
26. Hammer-butt flange	55. Stop rail and bumper felt
27. Damper-lever flange	56. Auxiliary-guide rail
28. Damper-lever spring	57. Auxiliary-guide rail screw
29. Damper lever	58. Auxiliary-flange screw
30. Hammer-butt spring	59. Auxiliary-wippen flange

sounds not required in the music at any given moment. Used in conjunction with the right-hand foot pedal, it is also a sustain arrangement, whereby the piano player can prolong or sustain any number of notes for any length of time required by written music.

In a vertical piano the damper heads and felts (and associated parts) are assembled as one unit with the hammer-action assembly inside the case. The entire affair is installed and can be removed as a single unit. See Fig. 4 for this portion of the damper-action assembly.

Each individual damper is operated through the hammer-action assembly by an individual key. The damper felt lifts away from the string or unison and remains in that position as long as its associated key is depressed. When the key is released, the damper felt once again contacts the string (or unison) and damps or silences the tone. The action of the damper levers is closely coordinated to the movement of the hammers. By removing the bottom door of the piano, one can view the rods and levers (trapwork) used to connect the damper-action assembly with the necessary foot pedal or pedals. When operated by the foot pedal, the damper-action assembly lifts all dampers at the same instant, and all notes played are sustained until the pedal is released.

In a grand piano the damper-action assembly operates according to the same principles as those found in the vertical piano. But the shapes and arrangement of parts are considerably different. Also, the damper-action assembly in the grand piano is completely separate (physically) from the hammer-action assembly. They are installed and can be removed as separate units. Of course, they are regulated and timed together. If you lift the lid of a grand piano, the row of felted damper heads will be seen in position on top of the piano strings. Depress a piano key and watch what happens. Now depress the right-hand foot pedal: all of the dampers should rise at once.

10. THE PIANO PEDALS

A. *Is a piano with three pedals a better-built instrument than a piano with two pedals?*

This is a commonly held belief that has no basis in fact. The number of pedals on a piano in no way indicates the quality of the instrument as a whole.

Piano pedals are supposed to perform functions necessary in the performance of piano music. Whenever a pedal does not perform an important function, it is relatively unnecessary. Many excellent instruments have but two pedals: a soft pedal and a sustaining pedal. Some inferior pianos have three pedals; in some instances the center pedal has no important function at all. Certain market-conscious European manufacturers put two pedals on pianos (including grands) destined for use on their own continent, but for export to America they add a third pedal.

It is important to examine the functions of pedals on the piano before you buy it, not because it will indicate the quality of the instrument but rather because it will acquaint you with the use of the pedals on the particular piano that you are buying!

Pedal use on all pianos is quite similar, but it is not always exactly the same.

B. *Is it correct to call the sustaining pedal the "loud" pedal, or "damper" pedal?*

The pedal on the right-hand side of the assembly is by definition and function a sustaining pedal. Its function is to prolong the sounding of a note or notes, not to make any of them individually louder. In fact, when a note or notes are played with the piano dampers lifted (pedal depressed), the sound is loudest immediately after the hammer impact, then it gradually fades away.

While the foregoing is technically correct, increased overall

31

volume can be attained in a musical passage by playing a *greater number of notes* while the pedal remains depressed. When all these sounds are sustained together, we have increased overall volume.

If you wish to call the sustaining pedal the "loud" pedal, it is doubtful that you will encounter much opposition. The same thing applies to calling it the "damper" pedal. After all, it does operate the dampers. The important fact to remember about this pedal is that its use activates *all of the dampers* on the piano *all at the same time.* It is found on all pianos.

There is another much less important sustain system used in some pianos in addition to the overall sustain of the right-hand pedal. It is activated by the center pedal, and involves only the bass dampers as a separate unit. This separate bass sustain is not necessary to the playing of good piano music. It is an extra, and is found on a great many American made pianos, both vertical and grand.

C. *How does the soft pedal operate?*

The pedal on the *left* (vertical or grand) is the soft pedal. Its name explains its function.

In a vertical piano the soft pedal is connected, through a series of levers and rods, to the underside of the hammer rail. (See part 40, Fig. 4.) When the soft pedal is depressed, a long dowel pushes the hammer rail and all the hammers closer to the strings. Remember, the shorter the blow of the hammer against the strings, the softer the sound. This movement of the hammer rail is adjustable.

The operation of this pedal (as well as the other pedals) should be noiseless. Check this in pianos while shopping. Usually a few minor adjustments are all that is necessary to silence irritating noises in this assembly. (A few old-time makes of grands used a similar soft-pedal arrangement.)

In a grand piano the soft pedal operates a series of levers and rods connected to a strong cast-iron lever that projects upward

Fig. 5

TYPICAL CASE PARTS of a MODERN GRAND PIANO
SHOWING LOCATION and NOMENCLATURE

1. Pedals
2. Lyre
3. Keybed
4. Keyslip
5. Fallboard
6. Music desk
7. Hinge (continuous)
8. Front (folding) lid
9. Back-lid log

10. Back lid
11. Lid prop (long)
12. Lid prop (short)
13. Top hinge
14. Case rim (outer)
15. Leg
16. Caster
17. Lyre brace

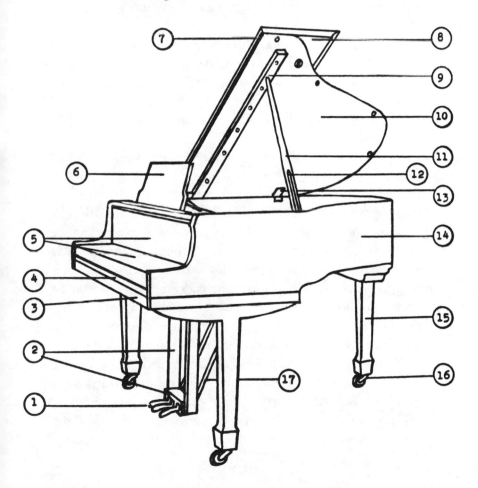

through an opening in the bottom of the keybed. The cast-iron lever is so positioned that when the soft pedal is depressed, the lever moves the entire keyboard assembly and piano action a set distance, usually to the right. (Depress the pedal and watch the keyboard move.)

With the soft pedal held down, the hammers in the grand piano action can contact only two strings in a three-string unison (note) and only one string in a two-string note. When the hammers contact *fewer* strings, we have a softer sound. When the soft pedal is released, the keyboard assembly and piano action are forced back to their normal positions by a heavy steel spring located inside the case at one end of the key frame.

A careful shopper should make sure that the pedal works easily and quietly and that the keyboard assembly and action move quietly and smoothly to the right, with a prompt, full return. If this operation is noisy, jerky, or without a full return to normal position, call it to the piano dealer's attention. It will need correcting.

D. *Is it necessary to have a sostenuto or center pedal on a grand piano?*

Years ago, sostenuto pedal assemblies were built into some large uprights in much the same manner as they are still built into some of the higher-quality grand pianos of today. The use of the sostenuto in the uprights was discontinued, and there is some doubt that this pedal assembly is really needed in grands today, except by a few top-flight concert artists. It can be helpful in interpretations of a few classical compositions, but there is relatively little written music that requires its use. It is definitely not necessary to the playing of modern piano music.

Average-priced or commercial-grade grand pianos do not (normally) have a sostenuto pedal. This center pedal is used, instead, to activate the separate bass sustain unit as described in "B" above. Some manufacturers of grands have eliminated the center pedal entirely, feeling that musical need of this pedal is too minor to justify the added costs of installation. The average piano owner can easily do without it.

The *sostenuto assembly* is made up of the center pedal, rods, levers, etc., which operate a rather delicate and complicated mechanism located inside the case at the rear of the hammer action. Portions of this assembly are built into both the hammer-action and the damper-action assemblies. A sostenuto pedal arrangement allows the pianist to sustain any one note or any combination of notes (those with dampers) simply by striking the keys, then depressing the center pedal to sustain these *selected* notes, while he continues to perform a musical passage wherein the rest of the music is not sustained.

If you entertain any doubt as to whether you will need a sostenuto on the grand piano that you intend to purchase, consult your piano teacher. If you are seriously considering a career as a concert pianist, it might be to your advantage to become familiar with the use of this pedal assembly.

E. *What are other uses of the center pedal?*

The center pedal on a *vertical* piano is sometimes used in other ways. It can be used as a means of lowering and raising a silencer (a long strip of thin felt, which when placed between the piano hammers and the strings, damps or mutes all but a small portion of the sound). Thus a person can practice in comparative quiet. If somebody in the house or in the next apartment works nights and sleeps days, he'll value this attachment. It is there to promote piano sales, but it can be useful.

The center pedal also may be used as a means of lowering and raising a mandolin attachment between the piano hammers and the strings much in the manner of the silencer. This item does not require a pedal for use. It can be installed with a cable control mounted under the keybed. Another type is positioned by lifting the piano top and adjusting the mandolin attachment by hand.

The center pedal is often used as an "extra-soft" pedal

Fig. 6

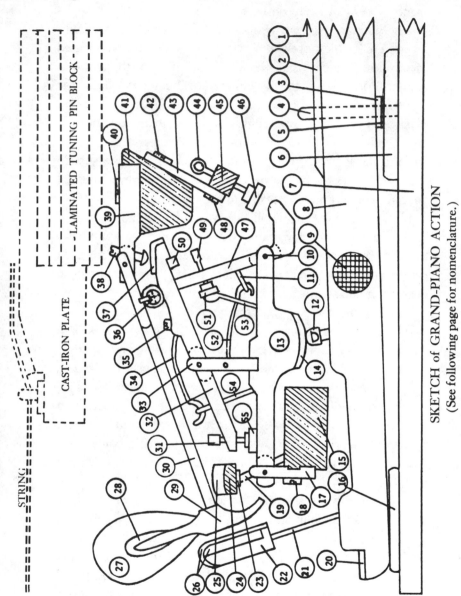

STRING

CAST-IRON PLATE

LAMINATED TUNING PIN BLOCK

SKETCH of GRAND-PIANO ACTION
(See following page for nomenclature.)

1. Front rail and assoc. parts
2. Key button
3. Balance-rail punching (felt)
4. Balance-rail pin
5. Balance-rail punching (paper)
6. Balance rail
7. Key frame
8. Piano key
9. Key leads (weights)
10. Center pin and bushing
11. Jack-spring cord
12. Capstan screw
13. Wippen or support
14. Wippen or support cushion
15. Wippen or support rail
16. Back-rail felt
17. Wippen or support flange
18. Wippen-flange screw
19. Threaded-rest rail support
20. Underlever-key cushion
21. Backcheck wire
22. Backcheck
23. Rest-rail adjustment nut
24. Hammer-rest rail
25. Hammer-rest rail felt
26. Backcheck cushion
27. Hammer felt (outer)
28. Hammer felt (inner)
29. Hammer molding
30. Hammer shank
31. Repetition-lever regulating screw
32. Repetition lever
33. Repetition-lever flange
34. Repetition-lever spring
35. Repetition-lever spring tensioning screw
36. Knuckle or barrel
37. Repetition-lever cushion
38. Dropscrew
39. Hammershank flange
40. Hammershank flange screw
41. Hammer rail
42. Regulating-rail support screw
43. Regulating-rail support
44. Letoff-regulating screw
45. Regulating rail
46. Regulating button
47. Jack or fly
48. Regulating-rail screw
49. Jack-regulating screw
50. Repetition felt
51. Jack-regulating button
52. Jack spring
53. Wippen spoon
54. Repetition-lever spring cord
55. Repetition-lever regulating button

(pianissimo). In this installation both the left and the center pedals are connected into the same soft pedal assembly to obtain differing degrees of softness. One is tempted to suspect that this system is a way to put three pedals on a piano without having any of them appear to be completely useless. This is a sales device that has found great favor with manufacturers and retailers alike, but it is a gimmick, and it will do little or nothing for your music. It is quite unnecessary: the pianist can depress the left (soft) pedal and obtain any required degree of pianissimo simply by lessening the force with which he strikes the keys.

11. THE LONG AND THE SHORT OF IT

Why is the volume of sound so much weaker in the extreme octaves of the piano?

This is a question that everyone, sooner or later, will ask. Please refer once more to Fig. 3.

You will note that the overall lengths of the strings gradually decrease as the piano scale progresses from the low bass to the high treble. Along with this decrease in length, the strings also decrease in thickness (gauge) as we progress up the scale. Shorter, thinner strings that are tuned progressively higher in pitch vibrate at ever higher rates of speed, thus lessening sound that is perceptible to the human ear. If the pitch rose high enough, we could not hear it at all.

You must realize that the sounding board of the piano is less responsive near its edges, where it is glued to the piano back or liner. The treble bridge (part 14) at its highest point is quite near the upper right corner of the soundboard (part 15). Vibration and volume of sound is muted at this point.

Differences in high-octave volume among different pianos is governed or influenced by scale design, size, and overall quality. Sometimes a competent piano tuner-technician can improve the tone volume in the highest treble, but not beyond the maximum volume of sound that was built into the piano.

Some of the above factors also apply to the loss of sound among the lowest bass notes, only the string length and thickness factors are reversed. The lowest tones can be muddy, with true pitch very hard to hear. The lowest bass string vibrates very slowly: at the rate of 27.5 cycles per second. The highest note, 88, vibrates at 4,186.4 cycles per second. Many people with a degree of hearing loss cannot hear either extreme. You can't always blame the piano.

When it is desirable to increase the overall volume of sound produced by a vertical piano, you can raise the top (lid), much the same as you would on a grand piano. Top-lid supports are found at one or both upper ends of the piano case. They are standard on most vertical pianos.

The Piano: A Complex Mechanism

The hammer and key action parts listed under Fig. 6 for the grand-piano action are all essential for playing just *one note* or *one tone* on the piano. If any of this array of wood, felt, leather, and metal becomes worn, corroded, broken, or otherwise out of regulation, the note may fail to play properly, if at all. There are enough other related parts in the conventional grand (or vertical) piano to total over 100 parts necessary to the correct production of each note. If we multiply this total by 88 notes or tones, we arrive at a staggering total of 8,800 piano parts: all of which must be in good regulation and repair if the piano is to operate properly.

When you consider that thousands of piano makes, with thousands of variations in parts and assembly, are in use throughout the world today, you may more fully appreciate the wisdom of hiring a fully competent piano tuner-technician to service your piano.

PART TWO

Purchasing a New Piano

12. THE PIANO WARRANTY

The standard piano warranty issued by American manufacturers claims or implies that a new piano is free of factory defects at time of purchase. It also guarantees that the manufacturer will honor the warranty for a specified length of time. During this warranty period, should a factory defect become evident, the manufacturer promises to either repair or replace the instrument, *subject to certain conditions*. Be certain that you understand the conditions. One of them may state that if factory repair or replacement is deemed necessary under the warranty, the cost of shipping the piano both ways must be borne by the piano owner. This is a legitimate protection for builders of fine-quality pianos; but it becomes an outright evasion of responsibility where it concerns the manufacturers of some of the "junk" pianos assembled today. A smart buyer will stay away from the "cheap" piano, no matter how nicely its polished cabinet shines.

Legally, the piano buyer is required to care for the piano according to the manufacturer's recommendations, or his warranty could become worthless within a few months. He can invalidate his piano warranty (and thousands of new piano owners do so) through his own neglect. This happens in nine out of ten cases within twelve months after the piano is purchased.

Ask the piano retailer to show you the warranty and *the manufacturer's booklet of service recommendations* before you make the purchase. A few minutes' studying them could save you from future grief.

Builders of the world's finest pianos recommend from two to four tunings a year for their instruments. By what strange twist of the imagination do piano owners (with the encouragement of many dealers) suppose that a moderately priced, run-of-the-mill piano needs less service than the well-built, high-quality instruments?

There are many piano retailers who conveniently neglect to give piano buyers either the printed warranty or the manufacturer's booklet of recommendations. Another questionable practice is the offer to "file" the warranty at the store. Politely but firmly decline such an offer. Ownerships change hands; stores go out of business. Where it concerns a piano warranty, *self-protection* is the name of the game.

Above all, do not take the piano salesman's unsupported word regarding recommended care of the piano. He is hired to sell pianos, not to service them. His primary interest is in getting your signature on a sales contract. The piano dealer who soft-pedals future piano service needs is usually the type of dealer who will refuse to honor your piano warranty should the need arise. His grounds? You failed to care for your piano as recommended by its manufacturer. Such a dealer is guilty of misrepresentation. But you will not have his *sales talk* in writing. Get the manufacturer's recommendations in black and white.

Choice of a competent piano tuner-technician to service your piano is also important to your warranty. A well-trained tuner-technician may spot a factory defect or failure, whereas an incompetent tuner may not. Most qualified professional service people keep detailed records which could prove (in court, if necessary) that the piano has had proper care. Such records are invaluable should you find it necessary to test your piano warranty.

13. YOUR APPROACH
TO THE PIANO MARKET

If you find yourself viewing today's piano market with a certain degree of confusion and trepidation, it may help to know that you are not alone. The days when a potential buyer could look at a familiar, nationally famous brand name and know with some certainty that he was seeing a good-quality, commercial-grade piano is long past. Certain assembly-line-oriented producers of today (on the trail of quick profits); cost-cutters, price-slashers, and fly-by-night keyboard touts; and high-finance groups that move in on a floundering piano company cheapen the product and proceed to milk the once-respected brand name dry at heavy cost to an unknowing public. All of these freebooters, and many more, have taken toll of the public confidence.

It is high time that a way be found to restore that lost confidence, to eliminate the causes and repair the effects, and an educated, well-informed piano-buying public is the force that will do it.

Meanwhile, there are a number of things that today's piano shopper can do to protect his interests (in addition to a thorough study of this book).

Let us divide piano production into two main categories:

1. Handicraft-oriented quality piano builders: piano makers who accept the additional costs of handwork methods when such procedures will ensure a better-quality product.

2. Assembly-line-oriented producers of commercial-grade pianos: piano producers who sacrifice known degrees of quality for the sake of machine-influenced standardization and lower costs of production.

All modern manufacture involves assembly-line techniques in varying degrees. The same is true of machine production. No modern piano factory could operate successfully without them. But when these elements are related to the manufacture of pianos, a difference in approach does exist.

We must also recognize some overlap between the two main categories listed here. That is, the lowest-quality (and lowest-priced) handicraft-oriented piano might, in some instances, be no better, or little better, than the best (and highest-priced) assembly-line-oriented piano of a different brand.

Handicraft-oriented quality-piano builders, who once represented the largest part of piano production within the United States, have through several decades become a minority. Scores of small concerns, unwilling to cheapen their products, have been forced out of business by unscrupulous competition; others have merged with larger quality-piano builders. But modern assembly-line-oriented methods combined with ruthless business tactics continue to plague the industry.

Handicraft-oriented quality piano builders (having chosen quality over quantity) make a limited number of pianos. Consequently, they cannot expect to stay in business if they build and sell defective merchandise. Each piano produced and sold must be among the best. This is part of your guarantee of a fine musical instrument. Another part of your guarantee lies in your acceptance of the manufacturer's service recommendations. *The finest piano manufactured in the world today, if service-neglected, will prove to be unsatisfactory as a musical instrument!*

One of the most frustrating and enduring obstacles faced by

generations of piano buyers has been the buyers' inability to find some sort of criterion with which to gauge piano quality. Resultant confusion, in many instances, has caused him either to conclude that all brands of piano are alike and then proceed to make a selection on the basis of price alone, or, regrettably, to lose interest entirely.

It would seem that *a guide to quality comparison* is mandatory if the piano buyers of the world are to have their day in court.

No two listings of brand names of present-day handicraft-oriented top-quality pianos (compiled by different sources) would ever be identical. The listing presented here is limited to American manufacturers and is represented as being neither complete nor without other fault. Its brevity is designed to avoid unnecessary confusion for the average piano buyer. *It is intended only as a guide or device to enable the piano buyer to determine—by comparisons—the qualities of other brands of piano, whether handicraft-oriented or not.* Each piano listed is universally recognized as a high-quality instrument; and each of them, widely distributed throughout the country, can be used as a basis for comparison with other available brands:

Steinway & Sons	Baldwin
Mason & Hamlin Co.	Wm. Knabe & Co.
Chickering & Sons	Sohmer & Co.

With a means by which to measure piano quality, you should be able to proceed with greater confidence. But use patience; don't be hurried. Make as many comparisons as are necessary to convince yourself that you are making a wise selection.

There are probably few among us who would not like to own a handicraft-oriented top-quality brand piano. But wishing will not make it so. Some of us cannot afford the initial cost of such an instrument. And we must consider a somewhat more speculative approach to the piano markets.

Assembly-Line-Oriented Producers of
Commercial-Grade Pianos

It was possible, not too many years ago, to divide commercial-grade piano quality into meaningful categories, such as: good, fair, poor, etc. This was before the freebooters, scarcely any of them piano builders, took over certain long-established firms and started the quality ball rolling downhill. Some of these profiteers even started manufacturing cut-rate "junk" pianos under new brand names. These people should be charged with littering, but as it is, we can only abhor the fact that lower-priced models of pianos manufactured and sold by long-established, reputable, commercial-grade piano producers are being forced out of the market.

Old-timers will recall that these quick-and-easy "money boys" are not new to the piano industry. They appear periodically, like a plague, usually in years of economic inflation. Back in 1929 (the year of the big crash) such operations folded by the score. It could happen again.

The average piano buyer is familiar with only a small percentage of the commercial-grade piano brands currently displayed in the market place. Once-respected brand names that he does remember are no longer in production. Others have been bought up and cheapened by outside interests as described. It is usual to enter a piano store these days and see inferior merchandise masquerading under any number of brand names that demanded considerable respect several decades ago, brand names that are now propped up only by former reputation and the money that new owners are pouring into national advertising.

By now you must realize that there is no rule of thumb for choosing a piano in today's commercial-grade market. *You* must be the judge. Make a thorough study of this book by way of preparation. Then consider for purchase only those models in the top one-third of any particular piano line. In this way you will practically eliminate consideration of today's junk pianos. And your chances of getting a fairly good instrument will thereby be enhanced. Incidentally, you also will be *serving notice* on the junk producer and his dealers.

Assembly-line-oriented producers ship out infinitely more "lemons" per one hundred units than do the handicraft-oriented piano builders. To add insult to injury, many assembly-line-oriented producers hold periodic "clearances" at the wholesale level—at which time they unload their most defective merchandise on certain cut-rate piano dealers in large lots at fantastic discounts. These retail "junk dealers" promptly set out to undermine all legitimate competition in their respective areas.

Such operations aren't too difficult for a piano buyer to spot. The piano "seconds" are usually unloaded on an unsuspecting public at some "factory-approved" sale or warehouse sale, or through the use of other misleading retail gimmicks. The faulty merchandise is peddled at cut-rate prices and a greater profit to the dealer than if he handled strictly first-line pianos. Such junk pianos are advertised and displayed along with a few good-quality pianos and sold as *new pianos* (which they are), *and no mention is ever made of the fact that they are seconds.* Junk piano dealers usually handle a great many different brands during any one year, and both they and their unscrupulous suppliers completely ignore *any* ethical franchise arrangements. Quick profits are their only concern.

A warranty? The smart operator offers one, confidently expecting you to invalidate it within a year through service neglect. This, along with such considerations as the victimized piano owner's reluctance to pay shipping costs to and from the factory for a defective piano, lets the dealer off the hook.

14. THE NEW FULL-SIZE UPRIGHT

Full-size uprights are no longer manufactured on a regular basis in the United States. But some foreign manufacturers build them and also smaller pianos. Prices compare favorably with good-quality smaller pianos of American manufacture, and many of the larger pianos are available in our country. Some of them have excellent quality and are sold with the usual warranty. One such make has a price range of $1,200 to $1,500 delivered to your home.

Some very selective piano buyers do not have room in their homes for grand pianos. These people are turning to the new full-size uprights to satisfy their desire for a deeper, richer tone.

15. WOULD IT BE WISE TO BUY A MINIATURE 64-NOTE PIANO ADVERTISED FOR SCHOOLS, SMALL APARTMENTS, TRAILERS, ETC.?

The miniature pianos are the sad result of a public demand for ever smaller, cheaper instruments. The only people who recommend them are those who make and sell them.

The miniature piano is notorious for its lack of stability. Some makes are worse than others; all are bad. Poor construction, too-short strings, too few strings to each note, faulty scaling, improper overall tension, disproportionate hammer velocity, and many other "bugs" too numerous to mention plague these disgraces to the piano builders' art.

The continued existence of these miniatures is dependent on an uninformed piano-buying public and its eternal quest for something for nothing. Don't be swayed by that time-worn salesman's pitch about Bach's having composed great music on a short-keyboard instrument. Bach's short keyboard was part and parcel of one of the best instruments of his day. Present-day miniatures aren't even distant relatives. Their sixty-four notes are parts of the worst pianos you can buy.

One finds that a great many owners of these ultra-small pianos are *not satisfied with their purchases.* And many piano service men refuse to risk their reputations by tuning or otherwise servicing these toys. Manufacturers of miniatures attempt to justify their products by claiming that they satisfy a legitimate public demand. This claim is without foundation in fact. Production of these units is just another way to make a fast buck.

For mobility in a school piano, purchase a good-quality studio upright (built to special school-piano specifications) with large, mobile, rubber casters. There are a number of brands on the market.

16. WHAT ABOUT THE NEW ELECTRONIC PIANOS?

Perhaps, some time in the future, the companies that are experimenting with these instruments will meet with a degree of success. At the present time, they have not succeeded in engineering an electric or electronic piano that sounds like a conventional piano. Furthermore, service needs of these instruments are many and varied. Owners may find it exceedingly difficult to obtain competent service through regular channels. In most areas of the United States, such service does not exist.

17. PIANO-ORGAN COMBINATIONS

A piano-organ combination is basically a regular conventional piano with the electronic organ notes (wiring and related components) added to it. All is enclosed in one case. Please see Item 18.

The piano-organ combination requires far more frequent tuning than a separate piano or a separate electronic organ. The overall pitch of a piano rises and falls with variations in humidity, heat, and cold. The overall pitch of an organ (although influenced) does not follow the same pattern. In fact, under certain conditions, the corresponding pitches of piano and organ notes may well be altered in opposite directions. This is hard on the musical ear. The result is a need for more frequent tuning (hard on the pocketbook). It is doubtful that piano-organ dealers will volunteer much prepurchase information on this point.

Tuning and repair services for your combination instrument may be very difficult to find. *Contrary to popular belief, most piano service men are not organ service men; and you seldom find an electronic-organ service man who can tune a piano.* There is also the fact that electronic equipment within the piano case obstructs work on the piano action, strings, bridges, and soundboard. Scant provision is made for this in the assembly of most of these instruments. They are a headache to service, and most competent piano or organ service people try to avoid them.

18. LITTLE-KNOWN TRUTHS ABOUT ELECTRONIC AND ELECTRIC HOME ORGANS

Some people prefer an organ to a piano. It is a matter of individual taste, and as such, it is of primary importance in choosing an instrument with which one can be happy. There are a number of facts that every potential home-organ owner should know. He cannot afford to be misled any more than can the potential piano buyer.

It is imperative to realize that you cannot really duplicate the musical tones that pour forth from a church pipe organ by purchasing an electric or electronic home organ at only a fraction of the cost of a genuine pipe organ. Yet, every day, home-organ salesmen tell customers that small home organs can perform this impossible feat.

Examine the following data on electric and electronic home organs. It will be to your advantage. Much of this data also applies to the larger types of electric and electronic organs sold to churches, schools, and places of entertainment.

The terms *electric organ* and *electronic organ* are not synonymous. They are two basically different types of organ. There is much public confusion regarding this difference.

A. An *electric* organ produces its tones through mechanical means, such as tone wheels, rotating disks, and steel or brass reeds—which tones are then electronically amplified. It is basically mechanical.

B. An *electronic* organ produces its tones electronically through the use of transistors or tubes in circuit with various other components. It is basically electronic.

All electronic organs must be tuned periodically if they are to remain in perfect tune. Some of these organs are very unstable (lower-priced makes) and require tuning and operations check quite often. Other, better, organs may go several years without tuning. Do not be misled by claims of "locked-in-tuning," etc. Electronic-tone generation is far from being infallible, as certain sources would have you believe. Electronic-tone generators (whether tube or transistor) suffer electrical change and deteriorate from excess heat, cold, humidity, general use, and age. An abnormal change in the electrical value of just one component among the many making up the tuning circuits can throw one or more notes out of tune. A good rule of thumb for electronic organs is to give the instruments tuning and operations check at least once every two or three years. (Electric organs employing reeds for tone generation must also be checked and tuned periodically. Reeds go out of tune for a multitude of reasons. A speck of dust on a reed tongue will cause a reed to perform erratically.)

There are only a few makes of modern home organs that need never be tuned. All are *electric* organs. One of them has mechanical tone wheels, others have rotating disks or other mechanical means to generate the various tones (which are then electronically amplified). These are relatively expensive organs. Caution: These same electric-organ manufacturers also build smaller (and less-expensive) home organs that are purely electronic. *Do not confuse the preferable electric models with the purely electronic models.*

Except for tuning, the electronic-service needs of both electric and electronic home organs are quite similar. (The latter, with more electronic equipment, is more prone to failure.) Both types have electronic amplifiers and a variety of electronic pickups, vibratos, tremolos, and electronic percussion attachments.

A potential buyer should consider that there is more electric and electronic equipment in some electronic home organs than will be found in ten television sets. This is something to think about.

What is the useful life of an organ?

The electronic components in the better electric and electronic organs, with little exception, can be expected to deteriorate, cause trouble at any time, and require overall replacement in ten to fifteen years (if you wish to keep the instrument in playable condition). At the end of this period you may be required to replace practically *all* of the electronic parts, at a cost equivalent to the price of a new organ. (Useful life expectancy of many low-quality home organs is considerably less.)

A fair estimate of the electrical-component life in a television set is eight to ten years (check with your television repair man), after which period it is cheaper to buy a new set than to repair the old. The chief differences between the electronic parts of a television set and the electronic parts used in an organ are the quantities, sizes, variety, and use. They will age in much the same length of time. Every potential buyer of a modern home organ should know what he is buying. Most people cannot afford to replace an expensive instrument every fifteen years.

Where can you get service for your organ?

This has become quite a problem for organ owners. There are many separate fields in the application of electronics (the field of organ electronics is a specialty). To be proficient in the service care of *all* makes and models of electric and electronic organs, a trainee must undergo years of highly specialized study. Every different organ model that appears on the market necessitates the use of a different wiring schematic (plan), a different approach.

Your local radio or television service man is not likely to be trained in this special field. More than likely he is not interested in it. Check him out before you purchase a modern home organ and expect him to service it.

Over the years the training of competent electronic-organ tuner-technicians has failed to keep pace with the potential need. The lack of trained men (becoming acute now when the organs sold a few years ago are showing troubles) could be laid at the doorsteps of the same organ dealers who claimed that electronic organs needed neither tuning nor specialized service. A final bit of advice: If you want an electric or electronic home organ, ask the dealer for an iron-clad agreement guaranteeing competent tuning and related service for the instrument before you buy it. You might also investigate the qualifications of any individual whom he recommends.

19. THAT SPECIAL ANNIVERSARY
OR STUDENT MODEL PIANO

These special periodic offerings from some piano manufacturers are the result of demands made by piano retailers for a cheaper product to put on *sale* (as a leader) to undercut the prices of their competitors. Such *special* pianos are almost always stripped-down models, with quality of manufacture cut to the bone both inside and out. Even the finish is likely to be inferior (cheaper lacquer or substitutes, or fewer coats).

20. SHOPPING ADVICE
AND THE PIANO TEACHER

Should you ask your piano teacher for guidance in the purchase of the family piano? Unfortunately, the answer to this question is certain to puncture the egos of a vast number of piano music teachers as well as shatter a myth long accepted as fact by the parents of piano students.

A piano teacher (teacher of piano music) does not really *teach piano;* he or she teaches people *how to play it.* There is a considerable difference.

Scarcely one in a hundred teachers of piano music has any concrete knowledge of the piano beyond the use of the keyboard and the pedals while playing the instrument. Tone preference is as varied among these teachers as it is among any group of music lovers, including the great concert artists. The teacher of piano music can offer the buyer little help in selecting a piano.

Now as to that myth. For years teachers of piano music (taken as a group) have basked securely in the knowledge that as music instructors they were beyond suspicion in regard to piano neglect. *The majority of them are unbelievably careless.* This statement may come as a surprise to many; but to the piano industry in general, the only surprise may be that somebody has finally rocked the boat. It is not unusual for a "piano teacher" to allow a piano to go for years without proper tuning. Conservative estimates indicate that at least 75 percent of the people engaged in piano music instruction cut financial corners by failing to keep their pianos in decent pitch and tune for their students.

Teachers of piano music who do not have their pianos checked and tuned several times a year (remember, they are teachers) are guilty of breaching the public trust. They are just as unethical as piano manufacturers who misrepresent their products, retail dealers who continue the process, and piano service people who claim professionalism and yet condone unworthy conduct by remaining silent. How can piano music teachers who neglect the tools of their profession be expected to educate piano students to do otherwise?

One of the greatest all-time mysteries of the piano business is the parent who naively sends his child to a music teacher to learn music appreciation on an out-of-tune piano. Is it any wonder that so many promising piano students become discouraged and quit? The average child student appreciates tunefulness; and when his teacher's piano (as well as the one at home) is out of proper pitch and tune, he soon loses interest.

This book has been written to give you the facts. Widespread piano neglect among piano music teachers is one of them. Assess a teacher's attitude toward proper piano care before you engage his or her services.

21. SHOULD YOU BUY THE SAME BRAND OF PIANO USED AND APPARENTLY APPROVED BY YOUR SCHOOL DISTRICT?

It is common practice for school authorities to purchase supplies by inviting dealers to submit bids. This practice cuts down on school operating costs. It also has value in getting the best deal from a number of dealers *who are selling the same brand of piano.*

That's the catch. Most schools accept bids on many different brands of pianos, subject to the same price yardstick, while little effort is made to evaluate the differing qualities of the piano makes offered. Much too often the low bidder gets the contract, regardless of the quality of the piano that he offers to the school. This is poor practice.

However, there are exceptional school systems (which emphasize piano music instruction or have exceptionally fine music departments) that do not follow the usual low-bidder routine They make a point of seeking quality as well as price. They usually buy good pianos, sometimes the best.

Whether you should be influenced by your school's choice of pianos depends entirely upon which of the above two purchasing arrangements your school follows. This might be a little hard to find out with any degree of certainty. I suggest that you learn all you can about pianos, then evaluate quality and price for yourself. Take your time. After you have narrowed the field down to not more than three brands, shop just as painstakingly for a *reputable* piano dealer. After a careful reading of this book, you should be in a fairly good position to choose wisely.

22. PIANO QUALITY
AND HOW TO SHOP FOR IT

We should make certain that the piano being considered is at the correct overall tension or pitch for which it was built to sound its best. The "A" above middle C should be pitched at 440 cycles per second. This is the American Standard Pitch to which all modern instruments are tuned.

The piano must be in tune. It is amazing how many pianos

are out of tune on the sales floor. One cannot make an accurate appraisal of tone in a piano that is out of tune. Sometimes an inferior instrument in fairly decent pitch and tune will sound better than a really fine piano that has been neglected.

The piano should be a console size or larger, offering us greater soundboard area with longer strings. It should have a direct-blow action fitted with *premium-quality hammer heads* that have not been treated with chemical reinforcing. The piano scale should contain an approved number of strings (see Item 8, B). Ideally, the piano should be a little heavier than average for its size (indicating a strong structural unit and a well-built case). All of these will contribute to better tuning stability, depth of tone, and volume of sound without distortion.

(Do not confuse *quality of tone* with *volume of sound*. In recent years manufacturers have been increasing the volume of sound in small pianos by the adoption of high-tension scaling. *High-tension scales* are widespread among spinets and consoles. This type of piano scale involves the use of heavier-gauge (thicker) strings, which contribute to a hard, brilliant, crashy sound. This undesirable quality is evidenced more in the spinet than the console piano, which has longer strings.)

There is a wide range of taste in piano tone, even among expert musicians. Good tone is a quality of sound that is pleasing to you as an individual. Brilliance or mellowness of tone are not constants. These qualities can be changed by a competent piano tuner-technician to suit the individual taste. (This procedure is called tone regulating or voicing and will be taken up in detail later.) As a rule, the manufacturer favors an in-between tone color that he hopes will satisfy the greatest number of piano buyers.

Resonance is another matter. This quality is built into the piano at the factory. It is the net result of how much research, quality craftsmanship, and material quality is put into the instrument *inside the case.* It cannot be improved once the instrument is built. Resonance is a constant, provided the piano is not neglected nor damaged.

Let us assume that you have shopped carefully and have made a tentative choice. Are you getting reasonable value for your money? To a very high degree, the price, as well as the quality of tone of a new piano, is governed by the quality of the instrument *inside the case.* Over 70 percent of the manufacturing costs of a fine piano are spent on the instrument inside the case. The manufacturers of low-quality pianos spend as little as 40 percent for the same purpose.

For your own profit and peace of mind, remember this: the manufacturer of the low-priced, inferior piano spends the greater part of his manufacturing dollar on *what you can see.* The builder of the better-quality, fine-toned piano spends the greater portion of his manufacturing dollar on *what you will hear.* This builder of good-quality pianos invests a great deal more in each instrument. He is entitled to ask and receive more for his product. *Pay a little more and get a lot more. There is no better way in which to invest your piano dollar.*

23. WHICH BRAND?

This is equivalent to deciding which make and model of automobile you should buy, only there is a much greater selection of piano makes and models than exists for automobiles. Invariably, you will make your own choice (as you should); and it will pay to remember that you really cannot get something for nothing.

The price ranges of the different models of each brand will give you a rough measure of quality. It may be necessary to do considerable shopping around to thoroughly acquaint yourself with the price angle. If you live in or near a large city, most well-known brands will be available for your inspection. If you live in a small town, your immediate choice of brands may be more limited. (But remember that buying from your home town dealer has its advantages.) Consider reputable dealers only. Stay away from the big (factory-approved) "sucker sales"; and avoid all dealers who offer an almost unlimited selection of brands.

Having finally decided on the price range that fits your budget, you can investigate the different available brands that fall within that price range. Examine every model of every brand. Your confidence in your own judgment will increase with every piano checked out. Right about now you will probably choose the model and the brand that you want (both at the same time). If you have studied this text carefully, you will have chosen the *size* and *type* of piano that you want (console, studio, direct-blow action, etc.) *before* you decided on the price range. It will be well to remember that searching out the lowest-priced direct-blow-action console model, for instance, that one can find may be no bargain either. Your choice should be a good-quality *musical instrument,* first, last, and always! And such a choice will involve a few extra well-spent dollars.

Now all that remains is to check out a number of individual pianos of the size, type, model, and finish that you have chosen. *Each piano is individual.* No two of the same model are exactly alike.

It is at this stage of the purchase that many piano buyers get "stuck" with an unsatisfactory piano. If the dealer does not have the exact finish that you want, *don't* agree to accept delivery of an instrument of the same model from the "warehouse" or "factory."

Insist on buying a piano that is already on the floor in the store, that is in correct pitch and tune, and that meets with your approval in every other way. Do not accept a duplicate model that you cannot see and examine before delivery to your home—a piano that may be at that moment stored in some cold, damp, or drafty warehouse, soaking up excess humidity and acquiring various other troubles that will cause you grief after delivery.

See it, hear it, check it out before you buy it.

24. HOW TO GIVE A PIANO A QUICK, PRELIMINARY CHECK WHILE SHOPPING

Look, but do not touch anything inside the piano. The piano dealer will appreciate it. If you cannot trust your children to keep their fingers off the merchandise (and this includes allowing them to wander about the display), leave them at home.

You will certainly think of additional items that you will want to check out; but here are a few things to remember:

1. Try all of the pedals; listen for squeaks and other distracting noises.
2. With the right (sustaining) pedal depressed, push down each of the eighty-eight keys in turn and assure yourself that they all return promptly to key level when released. (With the pedal depressed, the weight of the piano dampers is off the keys, making sticking or sluggish keys much more noticeable.)
3. Start at the left end of the keyboard and progress to the right, sounding each bass note (the copper-wound strings) with a firm but moderate blow on the key. This is a check for rattling or loose windings on the bass strings. Any such noises can indicate faulty strings. Loose windings normally require string replacement. (There are other methods of eliminating some of these noises when they are caused by poor stringing procedures—rather than by loose windings—but a new piano should not require their use.)
4. Ask the sales person to open the piano lid (top), also the

bottom door (vertical pianos). The latter is usually held in place by a couple of springs that are located under the keybed. (If there are still wooden wedges or blocks nailed to the underside of the keybed to hold the bottom door secure for shipping, you can rest assured that the dealer has not taken the trouble to check the instrument out. Maybe tuned; but checked out—no.) Look inside. Ask the sales person questions about what you see. This is one way of finding out if the salesman knows what he is talking about, or if he is just giving you a smooth "snow-job." Can he talk piano, or does he hedge and just talk prices? If he isn't interested enough in pianos to really know something about them, he shouldn't be selling them.

(Don't be too docile or timid to do these things. If you purchase the piano, *you will be paying for it.* Before you buy a car, you have the right to look under the hood and ask questions. You have the same right when shopping for a piano. A piano is a pretty substantial purchase. A piano salesman who knows pianos as he should will be glad to oblige you. It will give him a chance to really discuss the piano with you.)

5. Make certain that the piano is in tune, and at the proper A-440 cycles-per second pitch. The dealer should have a tuning standard at hand to reassure you on this point. A piano can be in tune with itself and still be incorrectly pitched. (See Item 46.)
6. Is the piano action responsive? Either play the instrument, or have a friend who is a pianist play it for you.

Be willing to listen to advice, *but make your own decisions regarding the actual choice and purchase.*

25. SHOULD A NEW PIANO BE TUNED BEFORE OR AFTER DELIVERY TO THE BUYER'S HOME?

The new piano should be at American Standard A-440 cycles-per second pitch and in good tune when it is shown to you on the sales floor. *Insist on this.* How else can you gauge its true quality of tone?

If the piano passes muster, you purchase it, and it is delivered to your home, a period of three to six weeks should elapse before you have it tuned again. This waiting period is necessary for the piano to acclimatize to its new location. There is always some atmospheric change, and the piano should be given a chance to adjust to it.

This procedure of waiting three to six weeks after delivery of the piano to the new location before tuning it is recommended only if the piano was at correct pitch and in good tune when delivered. If the buyer and the dealer slipped up on this for any reason, the new instrument should be pitched and tuned within a few days after delivery—to be followed by another tuning six weeks later.

The work should be done by a competent piano tuner-technician, and within the time period recommended. If you fail in this, you are off to a very bad start.

Who pays for the initial tunings (you or the dealer)? This will be governed by the purchase agreement that you make with the dealer. *Accept no oral agreement.* Get it in writing, specifying the time limits for any free tunings. You might be glad that you did so.

Always insist that your piano be tuned up to American Standard A-440 cycles-per-second pitch.

PART THREE

Purchasing a Used Piano

We can group used piano buyers into two general categories:
(a) Buyers willing to pay fair prices for good used instruments, and (b) the misinformed, who believe that they can obtain worthwhile used pianos for little or nothing.

Buyers in category "a" have a reasonable chance to acquire good used pianos. But the vast majority of buyers fall within category "b," and they usually get "stuck" with broken-down instruments that belong in the nearest garbage dump.

The demand for good used pianos always seems to exceed the supply. The situation today is acute, for many of the countless thousands of uprights and grands manufactured during the boom years prior to 1930 are long overdue at the piano graveyards. Owner neglect and age have taken their toll.

26. DEALING WITH THE PRIVATE OWNER

Most used pianos are put on the market by private owners. In general, these owners overestimate both the dollar value and the quality value (condition) of the instruments.

An intelligent home buyer has the house inspected and appraised before investing. This procedure should apply equally to the purchase of a used piano offered by a private owner. Hire a competent piano tuner-technician to examine and appraise the piano before you buy it. If the prospective seller is reluctant to allow this procedure, forget his piano and look elsewhere.

27. BUYING FROM THE PIANO DEALER

Piano stores sometimes offer used pianos for sale. Be careful when buying a used piano from any source, including the piano store. As stated previously, we have reputable piano dealers in this country. We also have some of the other variety. Your choice of a piano dealer when you shop for a used piano is just as important as your choice of a dealer when you shop for a new piano. It's easier to change dealers than it is to change pianos.

Used piano offerings are often used simply as "bait" advertising, even by some otherwise very reputable dealers. The main objective is to increase store traffic with the intention of selling new pianos, not used ones. The dealer doesn't really wish to sell his bait. He would be forced to find more (to continue his fishing expedition), and this isn't always so easily done. Therefore, he probably has his used pianos overpriced to protect himself. If he can sell one to you, he is likely to profit handsomely either way.

Actually, it is considerably riskier to buy a used piano from some dealers than it is to buy a used instrument from a private party, provided you have a competent appraisal made of the privately owned instrument. It is next to impossible to retain the services of a reputable piano tuner-technician to appraise a used piano at a store. The business-wise piano service man is very much aware that honest appraisals of most dealers' used piano offerings would inevitably earn him the enmity of these dealers.

Your piano dealer's *piano service department* is extremely important in conjunction with the purchase of your piano, new or used. Some well-established dealers have qualified repair shops of their own. Other reputable concerns hire equally reputable independent piano shops or individuals to restore their "trade-ins." A store of this type is preferred for a good used piano buy.

However, the vast majority of piano retailers in this country maintain no qualified piano service departments as such, nor do they retain the services of qualified piano service men. This type of dealer either makes no attempt to repair or restore used pianos, or he grudgingly calls in a part-time amateur or charlatan to do a quick, cheap job of "making all the keys work," and that is about it.

28. BUYING FROM THE
INDEPENDENTLY OWNED PIANO SHOP

A well-equipped, professionally staffed piano repair and re-building shop is by far the best source of good used pianos. Here you will find every piano repaired, reconditioned, or completely rebuilt by expert piano craftsmen. If there is a place where pride in craftsmanship exists side by side with dedication to the piano as a musical instrument, it is in the rebuilders' realm. Make inquiries. Perhaps there is such a piano shop, operated by qualified people, in your area. You can do no better than to look here. You may pay a fair price, but you will almost certainly get more for your money.

In many instances, these independently owned and operated shops also act as the piano service departments of the more reputable dealers in a given area. Such dealers are willing to pay a fair price for good work. These are the piano dealers who offer genuinely good used pianos for sale in their stores.

29. DISCONTINUED PIANO BRANDS

A great many brand-name pianos from the past are no longer manufactured. Do not allow this to hinder your search for a good used instrument. Whether an old-time brand-name piano is still built in the factories or whether some other piano make was discontinued has little significance when considering the purchase of a good used instrument. Piano brands among the older makes were discontinued for many reasons other than lack of quality. (For consideration of piano age, see Item 30.)

During the early part of this century, American piano-building experienced an unprecedented boom. This was brought about, to some extent, by the wide appeal of the player piano. But pianos of all types were built and sold as never before. Piano factories blossomed throughout the nation almost overnight (some were the freebooters and junk-piano producers of that day). This was the heyday of piano manufacturing in the United States.

Then came the international financial crash of 1929. The piano industry suffered the same fate as other types of businesses. Factories folded by the score. The crash played no favorites. Freebooters and reputable piano manufacturers alike closed their doors. Some of the latter were builders of very good instruments.

Piano companies that weathered the crash through mergers and by other means bought up the manufacturing rights to many once-competitive quality brand names and continued building such pianos in their own factories. Thus some good brands survived, while others, equally as good, perished. Today, huge American piano corporations manufacture any number of once-independent piano makes: the quality-oriented piano builders maintaining separate manufacturing facilities for individual brands (to preserve individual qualities); while assembly-line-oriented producers turn out several brands on the same assembly line (in many instances, only the brand names make it possible to distinguish one "make" from another).

Many of the discontinued brand-name pianos are in use throughout the world today, preserved through good piano care; others can be restored to almost new performance through competent reconditioning or rebuilding.

The buyer should make certain that parts for the instrument are still available. There are instances where some makes, especially foreign imports, cannot be restored for this reason. Check out this point with a competent piano technician or piano tuner-technician.

30. HOW TO DETERMINE
THE YEAR OF MANUFACTURE

You may recall earlier mention of a piano-reference volume, *Pierce Piano Atlas*, which lists the names and serial numbers of over seven thousand makes of American and foreign pianos. Such serial numbers are found on almost all makes of pianos. A quick check with *Pierce Piano Atlas* usually will reveal the year of manufacture. This handy volume is available to piano service people and dealers through the piano supply houses. It would be nice to think that every competent piano service man has one at his disposal; it is a fine source of information on both present and past piano companies.

Serial numbers on the upright or vertical styles of piano are most often located on, in, or near the upper part of the metal plate inside the piano. Some serial numbers, especially on the newer makes, are stamped into the top surface of the tuning-pin block; others may be found on the upper back board (behind the piano).

Grand-piano serial numbers are usually found on the piano plate near the tuning pins or stenciled on the plate braces.

There are instances where the number is found on the wooden bracing or framework beneath the piano. Occasionally, a number is missing altogether, in which case no certain determination can be made of the age of the instrument.

When you wish to learn the year of manufacture of a certain piano—and this applies to used pianos in a piano store as well as elsewhere—find the serial number and phone your request to a qualified piano service man. He will usually be happy to look up the year of manufacture for you without charge.

31. THE RECONDITIONED PIANO

The deceptive term *reconditioned* is generally subject to a thousand different interpretations by as many people. Let us try to qualify the term somewhat.

Webster's New World Dictionary defines the word *recondition* as follows: "To put back in good condition by cleaning, repairing, etc."

Applied to the reconditioning of a piano this should mean a thorough cleaning, complete repairing and regulating of the many thousands of original parts of the instrument, so as to put the piano back in the best possible playing condition. It might include the necessary replacement of a limited number of old parts with new. It is seldom possible to really recondition a piano without some replacement of old, broken, or worn parts. The foregoing could be termed a *complete reconditioning*.

The term *partial reconditioning* is the real culprit. It misleads the used-piano buyer into believing that the piano has been extensively overhauled, which is seldom the case. Pianos can be said to be partially reconditioned (in a legal sense) whenever a few minor repairs have been made.

When you, as a potential buyer, are told that a piano has been *reconditioned*, ask the seller just what work was performed

67

and whether it was done by a qualified professional piano service man. Some used-piano sellers try to recondition the pianos themselves by doing a little vacuuming, cleaning the keys, and applying a little wax.

32. THE REBUILT PIANO

The term *rebuilt* is also a vague and much-abused term. To completely rebuild a piano would be equivalent to the manufacture or assembly of a new one. The expense involved in either project could be about the same. Complete rebuilding is almost never done on a commercial basis. Rebuilding projects might include pianos of historical value (museum pieces) or pianos of sentimental value (family heirlooms).

When you purchase a piano that has been "rebuilt" on a commercial basis, you are likely buying a piano that has been only *partially rebuilt.* Or you might say that the instrument has been extensively overhauled.

Partial rebuilding would differ from *complete reconditioning* mostly in the quantity and major importance of new parts installed.

Parts replaced and procedures of major importance in *partial rebuilding* might include most of the following, *plus a complete reconditioning* of all remaining parts:

1. A new soundboard, or full restoration of old one.
2. New bridges.
3. A new tuning-pin block, with new tuning pins and new strings.
4. New legs, lyre, etc. (grand).
5. A new piano action (complete).
6. A piano action that has been restored to "like-new" performance by the replacement of a majority of its parts.

The preceding list is by no means complete, but it should

serve to indicate the major differences between *partial rebuilding* and *complete reconditioning*. Minor items like new key coverings usually are included under either procedure.

33. THE STUDENT PRACTICE PIANO

Some unscrupulous dealers in pianos favor the use of this ambiguous term in "bait" advertising. The *student practice piano* generally turns out to be an old, broken-down hulk, unworthy of repair or tuning. Such klunkers should be discarded. The piano student, especially the beginner, should never be required to "practice" on such junk; unless, of course, the object is to discourage the student from the start.

34. OLD UPRIGHT PIANOS

Several million pianos made before 1930 are scattered about the country in homes, schools, churches, etc.

At least 80 percent of these neglected instruments are unqualified junk. Perhaps 18 percent are worthy of complete reconditioning or restoration. The remaining 2 percent, owing to proper care through the years, are still in good condition. Frankly, the buyer's chances of acquiring one of the latter are negligible. His best chance to own a musically acceptable old upright is with the 18 percent that are still worth the cost of repairs. Such costs for good work could range anywhere between $150 and $250. Although additional old uprights could be restored, at higher costs, such work is considered ill-advised unless considerable sentimental value is attached to the instrument. In most instances, the piano owner should look for a better piano, or if possible, set his sights on a new one.

It is always advisable to buy a good new piano rather than to *over-invest* in an old one. You might consider that a good-quality commercial-grade piano of the 1970s can be purchased for little more than a piano of equal quality cost in the 1920s. This seems unbelievable, but it is true. How does this fact compare with the inflated prices demanded for other manufactured products of the day?

35. RESTYLING THE OLD UPRIGHT

The cabinet (case) of an old upright can be successfully restyled to satisfy the public demand for a less-bulky-looking instrument. (Let it be noted here that the full-size upright or vertical piano enclosed in modern casework is much preferred by some very discriminating piano buyers. More and more new full-size uprights are being sold each year the world over.) But before any such restyling project is attempted, it must be ascertained that the piano in question is musically and mechanically worthy of such a facelifting. It is first and last a musical instrument! Only a well-qualified piano tuner-technician or a piano technician (as differentiated from a piano tuner—see Item 47) can determine this fact for you. Make no mistake about this.

Never attempt to restyle a piano on your own. It is equally inadvisable to hire even a professional cabinetmaker to perform the task. (An exception would be a cabinetmaker who works or has worked at his trade in a piano factory.) Thousands of basically sound pianos have been ruined by overconfident people with a smattering of woodworking knowledge. It is disheartening to all concerned to discover that a piano restyled by unqualified people is not and never was worth the considerable work and cost.

Get that old upright inspected and appraised by a fully qualified piano man before you commit your hopes and funds to such an undertaking. Then have a qualified piano man do the work for you. It will cost you less in the long run, and you will own a playable piano.

70

Before leaving the subject of restyling, we should clear up the mistaken belief that an upright or vertical piano can be "cut down" without destroying its usefulness as a musical instrument.

An upright can be restyled to give the impression or appearance of a smaller instrument, but it cannot be cut off, top or bottom, to lower or lessen its original overall height. The wooden section cut out of the casework in the upper front of the piano together with the use of mirrors, modern legs, music racks, etc., is designed to give the *impression* of less height.

The metal plate inside a piano extends from the very top to the bottom of the case. There is no practical way to shorten its height without weakening it and destroying its ability to withstand the terrific tension of the 230-odd strings. (A study of the illustrations in this book or a look *into* a piano will soon dispel any lingering doubt on this score.)

36. THE USED GRAND PIANO

A buyer's chances of acquiring an acceptable instrument are somewhat better in used grand-piano markets. But an incautious approach can be disastrous here also. Many available used grands are hopeless wrecks owing to years of neglect. These include many of the famous-brand name pianos. A very important fact to remember is that age, wear, and neglect take toll of even the most expensive and durable instruments.

But in general, the grand piano, compared with the vertical, fares better through the years. It is a higher-priced, better-built instrument, and more grands are purchased by people sophisticated enough to be aware of the value of proper servicing. Also, a grand piano is usually treated with greater respect as a musical instrument. Thus there is a greater percentage of grands that can be restored to usefulness (preferably those of original top quality).

It is important to remember that any piano, whether grand or upright, that was manufactured before the year 1900 is generally a risky proposition for any kind of restoration, if your object is to use the unit as a playable instrument.

Every qualified piano man receives requests to restore aged square-grand pianos that people acquire under the impression that these old boxes are valuable antiques. These people believe that, if restored properly, these old squares are better instruments than modern-type grand pianos. This is wishful thinking. The modern-style grand piano is much superior to the older square style in every conceivable way, just as a modern radio is superior to an old crystal set.

Restoration of square grands is very expensive for many reasons, and almost without exception, ill-advised. Too, there are very few qualified piano men, who, knowing what is involved, will consent to undertake such a project. In general, old square grands are not valuable antiques. They are just old, worn-out pianos of another era.

Whatever the age or style of that old piano that you are considering, have the instrument examined and appraised by a qualified piano man before you make any commitment. Even a seriously neglected five-year-old instrument can be a "dog."

37. USED SPINET
AND CONSOLE PIANOS

In the 1930s (when the full-size upright went out of style and smaller pianos were introduced on the market), the piano industry had an abundance of cheap labor and good materials —but also shrunken markets and financial anemia. In spite of the problems (small pianos were also a relatively new concept), the limited production of the industry at this time showed acceptable quality and a great deal of promise.

This was not so during World War II and the postwar

forties. Experienced piano makers were scarce; proper materials were often unavailable. The average assembly-line-oriented, commercial-grade piano built during this period was a product of inferior craftsmanship and substandard materials.

The fifties brought something of a boom. Market prospects were bright and experienced workers and good materials were once more available. Long-respected manufacturers polished up their brand names and the "Pride in Craftsmanship" posters in the factories, and they began to turn out worthwhile commercial-grade pianos built to retail at reasonable prices.

Approved quality in medium-priced (and even some lower-priced) pianos lasted well into the 1960s. Then the outlook changed again. Unscrupulous promoters forced their way into the expanding piano industry. The result was a flood of low-cost, low-quality, highly polished "junk" pianos, many of them displaying brand names long respected by the public. Within just a few years profiteers have caused more damage to the American piano industry than depressions, recessions, wars, and foreign competition combined.

This information is offered mainly to give some background surrounding the manufacture of small pianos since their advent in the thirties. In conjunction with the serial number of a particular piano, it could prove useful.

38. PIANOS DISCARDED BY CHURCHES AND SCHOOLS

You can take no greater gamble than to purchase or otherwise acquire such a unit. When a church or a school discards a piano, you can be almost certain that it is entirely useless as a musical instrument. See Items 21 and 42.

39. OLD PLAYER PIANOS
AND REPRODUCING PIANOS

The Player Piano

Basically, a *player piano* is a regular upright piano with all of the parts and accouterments necessary for normal hand-playing. It can be used as a conventional piano for lessons, practice, etc.

The player-piano case is a little larger than that of the ordinary piano in order to accommodate the extra bulk of the player action. One section of the player action is located slightly below and forward of the regular piano action; the other major section (bellows, etc.) is located beneath the keybed and behind the bottom door. If electrified, the motor would be installed in this area.

The player action is operated by reduced air pressure (partial vacuum); and it, in turn, operates the regular piano action to make music. The player action can be operated either electrically (a motor); or it can be operated manually (with foot treadles). It can have manual means of *expression* (soft, loud, sustain, etc.); or a portion of the expression can be controlled by the tracker bar and music roll.

The Reproducing Piano

A *reproducing piano* is basically an ordinary player piano (described above), but with certain rather complex refinements. It can be either an upright or a grand piano:

1. All reproducing pianos are electrically driven. A "player-pianist" is unnecessary to its operation.
2. Stopping, starting, and repeating the musical selection are automatically controlled.
3. All elements of musical expression (touch, softness, loudness, full or partial sustain, accenting, crescendo,

74

diminuendo, etc.) are dynamically interpreted, reproduced, and controlled by the reproducing player action itself, working under the supreme direction of the music roll.

Note: There are between 4,000 and 5,000 parts in a player action or reproducer action. These, added to the approximately 8,800 parts of the ordinary piano, give us a total of 12,800 to 13,800 parts in the player piano or reproducing piano. All of these parts must be in good repair and regulation if the piano is to operate satisfactorily.

It is amazing how so many untrained people can believe that they can "pick up an old player" and put it back into decent operating condition all by themselves.

Availability

From the late thirties through the fifties there were many old player pianos and reproducers available from private owners for little or nothing (usually for the cost of moving an old instrument that wouldn't operate and was considered to be a nuisance by its owner). During this period thousands of repairable player units were removed from player pianos and discarded so that the regular piano could be more easily tuned and serviced. Few people believed that the player piano would ever regain popularity.

Then about 1960, the demand for old players and reproducers began to rise dramatically. But by this time, most of the self-playing instruments manufactured before 1930 had either been junked, converted to regular pianos, or ruined by incompetent or "do-it-yourself" tinkers.

At the present time even old players and reproducers that are hopelessly beyond restoration are being sold at absurd prices to unwary buyers. Consider the following:

1. *Both the regular piano and the player unit must be repairable.* Ninety percent of the time the regular piano itself is a hopeless wreck, because of years of neglect. Remember: the player unit is designed to play the regular piano (just as a person might do). Without the regular piano, you have nothing.

2. In instances where restoration is possible, the costs of the technical work involved (plus materials) are substantial. The work is demanding, in time, effort, and knowledge. Present-day costs for work and materials (by a qualified player technician) might range around $200 to repair and recondition the regular upright piano. Costs involved in restoring the player unit might range around $350. Total estimated repair costs: $550 or more, and this figure does not include cartage to and from the piano shop. These costs would cover only work performed on the interior of the instrument. Rebuilding and/or reconditioning costs for reproducers (especially grand pianos) could run considerably higher.

3. Generally the qualified player-piano technician will refuse to "just patch up" these instruments. After many years of destructive tinkering by unqualified people, including the piano owners, these old instruments are generally in pitiful condition.

Consider yourself fortunate if you have a really qualified player technician in your area who can do the work for you. Probably no more than one out of fifty otherwise fully qualified piano tuner-technicians are trained in player work. The average tuner knows little about it and generally cares less. He is likely to avoid all service work, including tuning, related to player pianos.

Public interest in the player piano continues to grow. A few manufacturers are now building new ones for the market.

These are of console and spinet sizes. Prices vary from a low of approximately $1,000 (for a small, bargain-basement treadle player with only sixty-four notes and scanty construction) up to $1,800 for a player with eighty-eight notes, both treadle and electric operation, automatic start and stop, repeat, etc., and quality of construction comparable to that of a good commercial-grade conventional piano.

Today's player units are almost replicas of yesteryear's player units. The few improvements include: a more compact unit; improved materials—such as better rubberized cloth, hose, tubing, etc.; and a plastic unit-valve construction that allows for easier servicing and is more resistant to atmospheric changes.

Note: The plastic unit-valve construction described here is indeed more resistant to atmospheric changes, but these plastic units make up only the valve assembly of the full player unit. The remainder (major portion) of the player unit, and, of course, the regular piano itself, is no more immune to the ravages of extreme humidity and aridity than was the old upright player piano or reproducer. Proper care, including at least twice-yearly tunings, is necessary if the player piano is to function properly for any decent length of time. (See Part 4, "Piano Care and Service.")

40. PLAYER-PIANO AND REPRODUCER MUSIC ROLLS: NEW AND OLD; AVAILABILITY

Player-Piano Rolls

New music rolls for the player piano are readily available. Sources include piano dealers who retail the new players, and a number of independent mail-order firms that specialize in piano rolls. (Ask your piano tuner-technician.) Present prices of new rolls are little more than they were forty years ago. So it is advisable to buy new cuttings (rolls), not only because of price, but because of other important considerations (discussed below). All of the various brands of player-piano rolls can be played on the older players as well as on the new pianos.

New music rolls feature most of the old tunes as well as many of the new. These include ragtime tunes, boogie-woogie, blues, jazz, swing, square dances with calls, polkas, Latin numbers, Irish melodies, medleys, patriotic songs, marches, religious songs, classical works, childrens' music, Christmas songs, pop hits, and show tunes.

Most old rolls unearthed from cellars and attics are no bargain; but where a certain title is unavailable in a new cutting, one might gamble on it. Old rolls may have many faults:

1. *Torn edges.* This causes the roll to "track" unevenly, stop, repeat too soon, cause unwanted notes to play; it can cancel out desirable notes, and cause numerous other evils.

2. *Paper stretched out of shape.* The tendency of paper to absorb moisture is well known. Excessive humidity causes rolls to stretch unevenly during use. Later, while drying out, they warp out of shape. This causes tracking problems owing to the misalignment of the holes (perforations) in the paper and the holes in the tracker bar. Most player pianos, old or new, provide for automatic tracking, but these devices cannot do the impossible.

3. *Brittle paper.* Such rolls should not be used in spite of all temptation to the contrary. Small bits of paper and paper dust are sucked through the tracker bar into the valve system, where they plug up air passages and cause many player failures. It is sometimes necessary to completely disassemble a player action (older types) to remove such

foreign materials. With new players this same trouble may require removal and replacement of some unit valves.

4. Many people who offer old rolls for sale do not know that new rolls are available at reasonable cost. They also are unaware of the above faults. Prices asked may be exorbitant. You can buy new for less.

Reproducer Piano Rolls

From the late 1930s well into the 1960s reproducer rolls in new cuttings were unavailable. But in recent years, new rolls specially cut for the Ampico units, and also rolls for Recordo reproducers, are once more on the market. New cuttings for other makes of reproducers may also appear. It would be foolhardy, in a fast-changing world, to list sources here. Consult your piano service man for current vendors of these products.

At the present time, owners of reproducers (other than the Ampico and the Recordo) must seek out old rolls specially cut for their units wherever they can. These rolls naturally will be subject to the same paper faults listed above. Your local piano tuner or dealer may be able to put you in touch with collectors who buy and sell these items. Classified ads and visits to antique dealers may help.

Owing to variations in tracker-bar layouts (means of expression), rolls for reproducers were never standardized as were ordinary player rolls. Each different reproducing system, when used with full expression, demands a specially cut music roll: Ampico, Duo-Art, Angelus Artrio, Artecho, Welt-Mignon, and Recordo, among others, all require rolls tailored to individual needs.

However, regular 88-note player-piano rolls, including the new cuttings, can be played on reproducing pianos. Reproducers are normally provided with cut-off levers or other means of temporarily deactivating the automatic expression controls, thus allowing the instruments to be used as ordinary electrified player pianos.

PART FOUR

Piano Care and Service

41. THE GENERAL CONDITION
OF PIANOS IN OUR HOMES

As stated at the beginning of this book, there are almost 10 million pianos in existence in the United States. Only about 20 percent of these pianos are tuned with any degree of regularity. The uninformed owners of the remaining 80 percent fail to make any demands whatsoever for tuning or related service.

Our nation's working force of approximately 5,000 competent tuners performs about 2,500,000 tunings a year. Over 1,000,000 of these tunings are concerned with pianos that receive two or more tunings per year. This means that about 500,000 pianos are tuned at least twice yearly; and about 1,500,000 pianos are tuned but once a year.

Thus about 2,000,000 pianos receive tunings during any given year. When we subtract these tuned pianos from the total number of pianos in the country, we are confronted with the fact that almost eight million pianos go untuned each year, most of which are located in the nation's homes. They are neglected by their owners, service-wise, year after year, ad infinitum. Far too many people do not realize that an out-of-tune piano is no longer a musical instrument.

42. THE PIANOS
IN OUR SCHOOLS

The hundreds of thousands of pianos in our nation's schools suffer much the same neglect as the millions of untuned pianos in our homes, and for many of the same reasons.

At the present time, about 40 percent of the pianos in our schools are almost never tuned; about 50 percent are seldom tuned; and only about 10 percent receive any kind of regular service. Owing to this widespread neglect, it is costing the taxpayers of America tremendous sums every year to replace instruments that have deteriorated long before their time.

Even in the 10-percent group, piano service is blindly purchased, in most instances, on the same low-bid basis that characterizes the purchase of inferior-quality school pianos. Little effort is expended in evaluating the competency of the piano service people who submit bids. Usually the low bidder gets the contract, regardless of the quality of his service.

What would be your opinion of a school that hired its teachers on a low-bid basis, with little or no consideration of teaching ability? The competency of such a teaching staff might be questionable to say the least.

Among many schools that do not even bother to budget funds for piano care, one often hears the complaint: "But we can't find a good tuner." These school authorities should be mindful of the fact that the Great Depression of the 1930s (when school pianos were tuned for three to five dollars each, and schoolteachers were paid less than a hundred dollars a month) is over. Nobody savors the implication that he is living thirty-some years behind the times. But where it concerns care of school pianos, some well-meaning school administrators do so.

A school administrator who is sincere in his approach to school piano care should consult the yellow pages of his area telephone directories. Likely he will find several piano tuners listed under the heading "Pianos—Tuning & Repairing." If he will use a little of the same care in choosing a competent tuner or tuner-technician that he employs when selecting a teacher, he will invariably retain the services of a competent piano man. Professional-quality piano service is always available to schools that are willing to pay the nationally prevailing tuning and repairing fees for such services.

43. HOW FREQUENTLY SHOULD PIANOS BE TUNED?

Any make or style of piano, regardless of its use or location, should be tuned a *minimum* of twice a year. Years of study and observation by qualified piano service men in the field prove that pianos infrequently serviced deteriorate (tonally and mechanically) at least twice as rapidly as do pianos that have the frequency of tuning recommended by reputable piano manufacturers. This is as true of pianos that have been placed in storage as it is true of pianos that are used daily in the home.

Every piano, starting with date of manufacture, suffers from changes in heat, cold, humidity, and aridity. Pianos are delicate, complex musical instruments, not just handsome pieces of furniture. An occasional dusting and polishing of the outside is good for the finish; but it does nothing for *the instrument inside the case.* This is not piano care; it is furniture care.

If you treat your piano like a piece of furniture and neglect its care as a musical instrument, do not expect qualified, competent piano service people to fall all over themselves for the privilege of servicing your piano. Good piano service men take pride in their profession. Theirs is a demanding art. Most of them are also good businessmen. They are likely to decide that your infrequent calls for service are too time-consuming, unprofitable, and not worth their efforts.

Possession of a piano may be considered a luxury, but

competent and regular service for the instrument is a necessity. Tuning at least twice yearly, as recommended by piano manufacturers, will greatly increase your musical enjoyment. And equally important: these *minimum* service requirements will protect your original investment. If minimum service requirements were observed by the piano-owning public, the savings in replacement costs and the extension of piano life would be so tremendous as to be incalculable.

But piano owners must realize that all pianos cannot be kept in acceptable tune and mechanical condition with only the minimum recommended service. Each individual piano contains certain qualities, quirks, failings, and potentials inherent in its creation. *Every piano manufactured is an individual instrument.* All pianos do not respond exactly alike under similar service any more than all human beings respond exactly alike under the same medical treatment.

Some pianos require more care than do others, depending on the quality of manufacture, use or abuse, and ability to withstand changes in heat, cold, and humidity, changes governed by the climatic locations of the pianos in question. Each and every piano will react to these conditions as an individual.

There are many pianos in existence that will not remain in acceptable tune longer than a half-hour after being tuned by the most exacting and competent of piano tuners. These pianos should be repaired or discarded.

Many educated piano owners have their pianos tuned four times yearly, with every major change of season. This procedure is highly recommended by the builders of the best-quality pianos in the world. Many professional pianists have their pianos tuned monthly, biweekly, or weekly; and in addition to this, these top-quality pianos (when used for concert work) are tuned just before each performance, and in many cases a competent tuner-technician stands by in the wings ready to make emergency tuning alterations during the performance.

Do not be upset by the prospect of a minimum of two tunings a year for your piano. If you cannot afford the minimum required service for a piano (compare it with the annual service costs for your automobile or television set) you cannot afford a piano. It is as simple as that.

44. HOW OFTEN SHOULD A NEW PIANO BE TUNED?

A *new* piano must undergo a "break-in" period during the first twelve months in the home. Thousands of new piano owners, unaware of this important fact, start their new pianos on the road to destruction during this first year. (Please study Items 45 and 46 very carefully.) A *minimum* of three tunings, spaced four months apart, are urgently necessary the first year. Four tunings spaced three months apart would be better. This procedure is recommended by piano people to overcome stretching the new strings and to "set" the new piano parts that counterbalance the $18\frac{1}{2}$ to $20\frac{1}{2}$ tons or more of string tension within the instrument. If this procedure is not followed, a dropped pitch is certain, damage to the piano is probable, and additional costs for pitch raising and mechanical repairs is the net result.

45. SHOULD PIANOS BE TUNED AND CHECKED DURING THE SUMMER MONTHS?

Definitely *yes*. The modern-day answer to this eternal question is in direct opposition to advice given to piano owners by the piano service men of a generation ago. The much-voiced belief that pianos located in certain areas of high summer humidity should be tuned and serviced "only after the heat is turned on in the fall and before the heat is turned off in the spring" is as outdated as bearskin overcoats. Today, only piano owners who refuse to take advantage of certain advances in modern piano technology need worry about the "best" times of the year to have their pianos tuned.

To an enlightened and progressive piano owner there is absolutely no difference whether his piano is tuned and serviced in the fall, winter, spring, or *summer*.

There are two main reasons why pianos that have undergone the proper "break-in" period, are structurally sound, not abused, and are tuned regularly at least twice a year go out of tune: (1) Extreme variations in relative humidity, and (2) temperature extremes.

Constant playing is a contributing factor, but actually if a piano is well tuned and in good repair, it is not a major factor.

Extreme changes in relative humidity and temperature not only cause your piano to go out of pitch and tune, but they are responsible for an enormous amount of structural and mechanical damage. Climatic conditions vary widely throughout the continental United States, but it can be estimated that more than 75 percent of all climatic piano damage occurs during the hot, humid months of summer. Such damage takes the form of rust and corrosion of metal parts: strings, tuning pins, center pins, bridge pins, etc.; the swelling of thousands of wooden parts; damaged soundboards; excessive string tensions; warped and sticking keys; and a host of other evils.

Today an electric *dehumidifier* element, designed to fit inside the piano case, can be purchased and installed for a reasonable cost. Such a unit is practically service-free. Ask your piano service man about obtaining one. It will be worth its weight in gold.

Ordinary room dehumidifiers have little effect on humid air trapped inside a piano. The special compact piano dehumid-

86

ifiers circulate the air that otherwise remains trapped inside the piano case, maintain a constant temperature, and are extremely effective. Installations of these units made during the past decade or so indicate that they may well outlast the normal useful life of a piano.[1]

46. WHAT IS MEANT BY RAISING OR LOWERING PIANO PITCH? HOW DOES THIS DIFFER FROM TUNING THE PIANO?

Raising or lowering piano pitch and tuning a piano to be harmonious are entirely different matters and they are done for entirely different reasons.

Lack of understanding in this respect is widespread among piano owners, and is responsible for an enormous amount of piano damage. A clear understanding of the difference between these two procedures is absolutely essential if the piano owner is to protect the investment in his piano.

From the moment the factory scale designer puts pencil to paper until the finished piano is crated and shipped, every effort is aimed at making that particular style of piano sound its musical best at one particular tone height or overall *pitch*. That target pitch is A-440 cycles per second, also known as American Standard Pitch.

This means that the string unison "A" above middle C on your piano cycles or vibrates at the rate of 440 times each second when struck by the piano hammer. (A unison is made up of two or three strings tuned exactly alike, located side by side, and forming the same note when struck by the same hammer. Almost all the notes on the piano are unison notes,

---

[1] Recommended use of piano dehumidifiers varies with condition of piano and climatic changes. Consult your piano service man!

with the exception of a few in the low bass that sound from heavy-wound single strings.) The individual tone heights of the other eighty-seven notes are obtained with reference to "A."

The overall pitch of a piano is the total overall balanced tension in pounds-pull of all of the 230-odd strings in the instrument. For example: In a typical piano each string, according to length, thickness, tautness, and location in the scale, exerts a calculated tortional tension or pull (in pounds) on the structural unit (back, plate, and tuning-pin block). The average tension or pull per string could approximate 170 pounds. When we multiply the average string tension by 230-odd strings, we come up with an overall string tension of approximately 39,100 pounds, or *almost 20 tons of tortional pull* within the framework of this piano.

Total overall balanced string tensions vary somewhat among pianos of different stringing scales (different makes and models). It might well be anywhere between 18 and 20 or more tons of tortional pull. Just imagine using the tremendous pull that is trapped within the average piano to power a hoist. Such a hoist could lift forty or more heavy, old uprights all at the same time.

It should now be apparent why the delicate task of lowering or raising the *pitch* (overall balanced string tension) of a piano is no job to entrust to an incompetent or amateur tuner. It should also be clear why "tuning quacks" seldom mention the matter of correction of pitch to a customer. It is much safer and simpler for them to tune the piano at the overall pitch that already exists, take the fee, and run.

Such practice allows the piano pitch to sink lower and lower, until the lack of proper overall balanced string tension results in serious structural failures in the instrument.

Where lack of proper care has allowed the overall pitch to sink a quarter-tone, the loss in proper overall string tension is

1,500 to 2,500 pounds. Where overall pitch has sunk a half-tone, the loss in proper overall string tension is 3,000 to 5,000 pounds. In many older pianos that have gone without proper care for years, the loss in proper overall balanced string tension can amount to several tons.

It must be remembered that when a piano is constructed, the basic structural parts (piano back, cast-iron plate, and tuning-pin block) are engineered as a unit to remain at their structural best *when holding up the correct overall balanced string tension.* Therefore, when the correct overall pitch is lacking, parts of the piano are apt to warp, loosen, crack, split, bulge, or otherwise suffer damage. This means loss in both the *value* and the *performance* of the instrument. If the damage is great and is sustained over a long period of time (several or more years), it can render the piano worthless.

Structural damage to the piano can be minimized by keeping the proper balanced overall string tension or proper overall pitch on the piano at all times. This can be accomplished only through frequent tuning to the pitch of A-440 cycles per second (American Standard Pitch). This means that you should have your piano tuned twice a year or more often, as recommended by the builders of your piano. Failure by the piano owner to follow these recommendations causes failures in his piano in proportion to the total neglect.

Many piano owners lack factual information regarding the above-stated needs of their pianos. But when they are aware of the truth and still neglect the care of their instruments, the fault is entirely their own.

Now that *you* are aware of these facts of piano life, it is hoped that you will no longer believe that a piano tuner is trying to "con" you when he recommends the minimum of two tunings a year for any piano. He is doing you a real service!

Other critically important parts of the piano, such as the

soundboard, bass bridge, treble bridge, and soundboard ribbing, suffer extensive damage from loss of overall balanced string tension. For example, the average piano string (loaded with about 170 pounds of tension) also exerts a secondary force against the bridges and "crown" of the soundboard. This *push* amounts to about 7 pounds per string. If we multiply this by 230-odd strings, we have 1,610 pounds of push-force against the bridges and soundboard of a piano pitched at A-440 cycles per second. To counterbalance this tremendous push-force we have the crown of the board and the curved ribs exerting force in the opposite direction.

When overall piano pitch is allowed to change too much, the balanced forces between the strings and the bridge-soundboard combination are upset. This results in damage to the bridges, soundboard, ribbing, and associated parts. Such damage usually takes the forms of warps, splits, cracks, or broken glue bonding on the bridges, soundboard, and ribs. These can be very serious failures.

It should be apparent why even the most reputable of piano manufacturers and dealers cannot afford to stand behind the warranty of a piano unless the piano owner takes proper care of the instrument.

In an overwhelming percentage of pitch-correction jobs the piano tuner-technician is faced with a loss in overall string tension (the pitch is dropped). But where excessive humidity has caused a formerly well-pitched piano to rise above A-440 cycles per second (which sometimes happens from high summer humidity), the piano is overloaded with tension. This *rise* in overall string tension, if excessive, can also damage the piano. Use of a dehumidifier element installed inside the piano is highly recommended, at least during the months of highest relative humidity. In some areas it may be necessary to keep a dehumidifier in operation all year round. (Consult Item 45.)

In the foregoing discussion we have been primarily concerned with the overall balanced string tensions in the piano (overall pitch). To review, note that changes in overall piano pitch are involved with hundreds and even thousands of pounds of overall string tension. When a piano tuner-technician raises the pitch of a piano a half-tone he is required to add from 3,000 to 5,000 pounds of overall tension to the instrument. He is dealing in *tension*. He is not at all concerned with sound, except to use it as a rough guide to estimate the proper tensions. So when he has finished adding the correct amount of overall *tension* to the piano, the instrument will still be out of tune.

But once the overall tension (pitch) has been corrected, the piano tuner can switch his primary objective to the *sounds* that the strings make when they are struck by the piano hammers. Until now these *sounds* mattered very little. Now they become all-important as the work progresses in *tuning the instrument into harmony*.

The tuner does this by adjusting the *sound* or number of string vibrations of each note to an exact relationship with the same factors of all 230-odd strings. He is dealing in differences in *sound* and variations in string vibration so infinitesimal that it is impossible for the untrained ear to detect them. Your piano tuner has switched from mechanical engineer to artist. He is conceiving beauty in sound waves in relation to the human ear. He will adjust and listen intently to the sounds of every string. In so doing he will be engaged in adjusting and making comparisons in piano string tensions, *but only in infinitely small fractions of an ounce per string;* and only as a byproduct of the exact *sound* that he must achieve. When he has finished tuning he will have 230-odd fundamental tones, each with its quota of lesser tones (partials) so arranged in harmonious relationship with one another within the framework of eighty-eight notes that only the presence of a pianist is needed to open the doors to the joys of music.

It should now be clear why your piano tuner makes a separate charge for *changing the pitch* on a piano; it should also be apparent why he makes a separate charge for *tuning* a piano.

A piano tuner can tune the piano at any one of a thousand incorrect pitches, and although the piano will sound in harmony with itself, the overall balanced string tension of the instrument will be all wrong, with possible disastrous consequences in ear training and piano damage. Also, a piano tuned to such an off-pitch cannot be played in tune with other fixed-pitch instruments.

The piano should be tuned to the correct pitch of A-440 cycles per second; but in order to tune the piano *to* this pitch, *the correct pitch or overall balanced string tension must already be in evidence.* If it is not, and the piano is basically sound enough to hold the correct overall tension, the tuner must go through the separate procedure of correcting the overall pitch before he can proceed to tune the instrument.

Both you and your tuner will avoid a lot of headaches by following the manufacturers' recommendations for frequent and regular tunings. The overall pitch will be maintained on your piano without additional costs, and you will enjoy the instrument a good deal more. Your piano tuner-technician must be capable of making overall pitch changes whenever necessary, but he is always happier when it is not necessary. In most cases he can tune another well-pitched piano in less time and with much less effort than he must expend in correcting the pitch on a badly neglected piano.

After a pitch-changing session and the initial tuning, a follow-up tuning in from three to six months is absolutely necessary to retain the added tension (the piano will react by settling after the first session). If the piano is allowed to settle too long before the follow-up tuning, another pitch-raising session (at additional cost) will be required.

47. WHAT ARE THE TRUE MEANINGS OF THE TITLES "PIANO TUNER," "PIANO TECHNICIAN," AND "PIANO TUNER-TECHNICIAN"?

There are some in the field of piano service who usurp these titles indiscriminately. Such practice by unqualified people is highly unethical. Each title implies the possession of certain skills, and all three titles have long been a part of the piano servicing profession. It will profit the piano owner to know their true meanings, the better to guard against incompetents and to choose his own piano service man. We are not concerned here with the factory definitions of the terms, but only as they apply to men engaged in piano care in the field.

A *piano tuner* limits his practice almost entirely to tuning pianos. He may or may not be capable of minor piano repairing.

A *piano technician* is a highly skilled piano mechanic. He is skilled in many or all of the delicate, complex procedures that go into reconditioning, restringing, or rebuilding pianos. His knowledge of piano technology should include the skills necessary for all major and minor repairing, including the installation of tuning-pin blocks and soundboards, key recovering, action rebuilding, action regulating, tone regulating (voicing), and perhaps refinishing, to name a few. His work is essentially shopwork; this may or may not include some ability to tune pianos.

A *piano tuner-technician* is a highly skilled combination of both expert piano tuner and expert piano technician. His extensive knowledge and abilities should include all skills related to the care and restoration of pianos.

48. IS COMPETENT
PIANO SERVICE AVAILABLE?

The well-informed piano owner who wishes to keep his piano in good condition through regular servicing has little need for worry on this score. Competent, professional piano service is generally available anywhere in the continental United States.

This does not mean that you will always find a "local" full-time, professional tuner based in a given area. Some small towns and rural areas cannot support a professional piano service man, any more than they can support a full-time physician, dentist, clergyman, or lawyer. In recent years the professional piano tuner has migrated to the larger cities, with their concentrated populations.

However, there are actually more professional piano service people prepared to meet today's piano needs (actual demand) than ever was the case in the past. It is simply a matter of knowing how and where to contact them.

Today, most of our towns, villages, and rural areas are serviced by city-based tuners who travel thousands of miles every year to take care of "outside" service needs. You will have to contact these professionals. They do not canvass the countryside, knocking on doors to ask people if they want their pianos tuned. Lack of understanding in this respect is largely responsible for imaginary tuner shortages and widespread piano neglect.

As an "outside" customer, you will be required to pay a reasonable amount (in addition to regular tuning and repairing charges) for the tuner's automobile expenses plus his time on the road. But it is standard practice among reputable tuners to split all traveling costs among the several customers serviced in one area on the same trip.

Therefore, it will be to your advantage to "buddy-up" with two or more other piano owners and arrange for tunings on the same day or trip. If the tuner must travel a long distance, requiring much time on the road, he may consider a trip just to tune one piano (which might be a wreck and not worth tuning) economically unfeasible.

It is also well to remember that many piano tuners run one-man service setups and operate out of their homes. Whenever possible, phone these tuners during the evening when they are more likely to be available to take the call.

Thus when it is time to have your piano tuned, consult the yellow pages of your local and area telephone directories (many tuners are listed in a number of directories). You are likely to find anywhere from a few to several dozen qualified tuners listed under the heading "Pianos—Tuning & Repairing." Place a call to the one of your choice and make your appointment. See Items 64, 65, 66, and 68 for additional information on this subject.

49. YOU CAN HELP YOUR PIANO SERVICE MAN DO A BETTER JOB

The following rules are important:

1. Try to provide him with a period of relative quiet to facilitate his work. All professional piano tuners realize that the customer's home life must continue during a tuner's visit. His powers of concentration are such that he can ignore most of the less-disturbing noises common to a particular location. But it is practically impossible for him to do good tuning with a radio or television set blaring in the house. Musical interference from another source distorts the minute comparisons and calculations of musical vibrations with which the tuner is engaged. Such interference is similar to electrical disturbances in a radio or television that cause sound or picture distortion.
2. Suppress the impulse to roll out the vacuum cleaner the instant the tuner opens the piano. The tuner cannot

afford to spend valuable time cleaning your piano for nothing. The fee for tuning a piano does not include the work of cleaning it inside or out. This is a time-consuming task for which he is justified in charging an extra fee. Cleaning the inside of a piano is a delicate task best left to the professional. There are thousands of small parts that can be thrown out of regulation by untrained or careless hands, resulting in costly piano regulating and repairs. If you think that your piano needs cleaning (a professional job), ask the tuner about it. He may or may not have time to do it that particular day, depending on his scheduled appointments. But a good tuner will do the work for you at his earliest opportunity.

3. *Please write down and remember the appointed day and hour of the tuning appointment.* Failure to do this happens more often than you would think. It is the ultimate discourtesy, and it practically guarantees a professional-piano-tuner shortage for the guilty party (if the word gets around).

4. Remove all knicknacks, books, pictures, and other items from the piano before the tuner arrives. This is your job, not his. A piano man's estimate of a customer always suffers when he arrives to find the piano laboring under the burden of a hundred pounds of assorted material (and no convenient place to put it).

If you will observe the four cardinal rules listed above, you will certainly help your tuner to do a more efficient job.

50. PIANO LORE—A PROTECTION

We all know that there are unethical and incompetent practitioners in every profession. Much as we who work in the piano servicing profession desire a system that would seal the loom of the unscrupulous tuner, dealer, or manufacturer, there appears to be no effective, short-term way in which to do it. A thoroughly enlightened piano-owning public seems to be the only answer.

Learn all that you can about pianos and their care. Widespread public knowledge of the piano, its construction, its wondrous mechanisms, and its musical and mechanical needs will do much to hasten the demise of undesirable elements in the industry.

51. THE AURAL (EAR) TUNER VS. THE USE OF ELECTRONIC TUNING AIDS

This is a highly controversial topic, both within and outside the piano service profession. Perhaps it will always be so, for electronic tuning aids do have their uses as tools connected with manufacturing pianos. But as efficient tools for tuning in the field they leave a great deal to be desired. A huge majority of aural tuners oppose the use of these electronic gadgets in the field of piano tuning.

In a space age devoted to missile firings and plans for trips to other planets, many people believe that electronic gadgetry can do anything. And today we have the usual crop of opportunists who are ready to take advantage of it. In the field of piano service, the negative effects stemming from the use of electronic tuning aids far outweigh the good.

Any survey of those people who adopt the use of electronic equipment as tuning aids will reveal the following:

1. A majority of the misinformed amateurs who enter the field each year on a part-time basis do so to supplement income from other sources. This is equivalent to purchasing a small x-ray machine and a pair of pliers and starting

practice as a part-time dentist. It matters little that these people, completely unschooled in even the fundamental aspects of real piano technology, eventually fold up their tents and steal away. What does matter is that they leave behind them an enormous number of improperly serviced and even damaged pianos.

2. People who simply lack the natural talents necessary to becoming good aural (ear) tuners. Square pegs are not shaped to fit into round holes, and sight-tuning can never compensate for God's gift of a fine musical ear.

3. Former successful aural tuners who have suffered a substantial degree of hearing loss; and who, either through false pride or economic necessity, refuse to hang up their tuning hammers and call it a day.

You may recall a bit of information contained in Item 43: "Each individual piano contains certain qualities, quirks, failings, and potentials inherent in its creation. *Every piano manufactured is an individual instrument.* All pianos do not respond exactly alike under similar service any more than all human beings respond exactly alike under the same medical treatment."

The accomplished aural tuner tailors his tuning to each individual piano. His every effort is aimed at creating musical "life" from each instrument's individual qualities and peculiarities. Electronic piano tuning aids are found wanting, even in the hands of highly regarded musical-research experts. The mathematically prescribed patterns of these machines dispense the same medicine to all patients, regardless of individual need. Such tuning is without character, and without "life."

52. MUST A PIANO TUNER BE A "PLAYER" TO BE A GOOD TUNER?

Because the art of piano tuning and the art of playing the piano are related to the same instrument does not mean that either the tuner or the pianist must be accomplished in both.

To judge a concert artist on his ability to tune pianos would be ridiculous. By the same token, a piano service man cannot be judged by his ability to play the instrument. Some excellent piano tuners cannot play the piano. Many thoroughly incompetent ones play quite well. To judge a piano tuner's ability to do his job by whether or not he plays the piano could be a costly mistake.

Although it is not at all necessary to good tuning work, it is nice if your tuner can render a selection or two on the piano, if only as a means of demonstrating to you the improved musical sound of the instrument after tuning. If the tuner is also a piano technician, this aids him in testing the overall performance of the instrument in relation to its numerous mechanical parts. Most tuner-technicians are quite capable in this regard.

53. SHOULD A REPUTABLE PIANO SERVICE MAN GUARANTEE HIS WORK?

If you have faithfully studied and digested the information already offered in this book, you now know that only the uninformed amateur, the hit-and-run tuning charlatan, or an outright fool would have the temerity to guarantee piano tuning or any other kind of service work connected with the piano.

The piano service man is in the same boat as the physician and the dentist. There are just too many variables involved with the incidence of heart disease, toothache, and the things that happen or do not happen to pianos. The extent to which many people risk their lives by ignoring expert medical advice and the extent to which so many piano owners neglect the musical and mechanical health of pianos offer striking similarities. The medical profession must resign itself to the fact that there will always be some people who will swallow a dose of medicine prescribed for stomach ulcers and then sit down to a lazy susan loaded with radishes, onions, and red peppers. If you were a doctor would you guarantee the health of such patients?

The piano service profession will always know of people who will neglect their pianos for five, ten, or twenty years; finally have the pitiful instrument tuned (expecting, of course, that one tuning will cure all of its musical and mechanical ills); then move the piano from a cold room into a warm room, or vice versa; allow the family preschoolers to hammer on the instrument during the three weeks it takes to get the television repaired, or let the kids play "tooner" with an old pair of pliers; and then call the piano service man and complain that "the piano doesn't sound right *since you tuned it.*"

An extreme case? Any professional piano service man can recall similar experiences. Not long ago, after tuning a beautiful and nice-sounding console piano just six months out of the factory, I stood in a doorway and bid a lady customer goodbye while her three-year-old son hammered gleefully on the glistening new keyboard with a heavy wooden toy locomotive.

54. THE REQUEST TO JUST TUNE UP A FEW BAD NOTES

A piano does not lose its correct tuning a few notes at a time. After studying Items 43, 44, 45, and 46, this should be evident to the reader.

The proper, balanced overall string tension, the basic overall pitch, and the exact tuning of each individual string on the piano are so interrelated that when the average ear can detect "a few bad notes" it is 100 percent certain that all of the notes on the piano are out of pitch or tune. For each note the extent of the error is only a matter of degree.

These *bad* notes indicate *that the entire piano is out of tune,* and a new temperament setting and complete new tuning is in order. A tuning will not hang together unless the tuner starts from scratch and tunes *all* strings at the same session. To ask a tuner to "just tune up a few bad notes" is an admission that you are tone-deaf, parsimonious, or both. It also is an open invitation to quackery.

A good, reputable tuner will not leave a piano until he is certain that the instrument will hold its tuning as well as it is possible for that particular instrument to do so. And when a certain piano has loose tuning pins or another ailment, he will inform the customer of these conditions that might cause future trouble with the tuning. In this case it is up to the owner whether he wishes to have the instrument tuned more often because of the defect or repaired to remedy the defect.

55. WHAT IS MEANT BY ACTION REGULATING?

Webster's Collegiate Dictionary defines the word *regulate* thusly: "To adjust so as to work accurately or regularly; as, to regulate a clock."

A complete job of piano action regulating involves the adjustment and timing of each of the thousands of parts that make up the mechanical unit: keyboard assembly, hammer action assembly, and damper-action assembly. (See Item 9.)

It is well to note that regulating specifications for the many different brands and styles of pianos are far from being uniform or standardized. Each manufacturer specifies his own measurements and tolerances. In many cases, older brands of pianos that are no longer manufactured must be regulated by "the feel of the thing," as specifications for these are no longer obtainable. This is where the men are separated from the boys, where the well-trained technician proceeds with confidence, while the less qualified either botch the job or decline the work.

A meticulous technician may well spend two days on a regulating project if the piano in question is a grand. If the piano is a vertical, both the time element and the cost of the work may be less. (Consult "A Service Fee Guide," Item 66.) However, any quoted fee for the work will be an *educated estimate*, not a hard and fast price. You should understand this for your own peace of mind. Individual pianos present individual problems, and costs will vary. No intelligent technician will agree to work under any other arrangement. Also, when action repairs, new key felts, or replacement of other parts are necessary, the complete job will take longer and be more costly.

Pianos go out of regulation for many reasons: normal wear to parts, excessive shrinkage and expansion of wooden parts owing to climatic conditions, warpage, loss of strength in hundreds of delicate steel springs, damage from moths or mice (which often necessitates complete re-regulating of the piano), careless piano moving, abuse, and general neglect.

New pianos are finely regulated at the factory before they are shipped. But even relatively new pianos are subjected to many of the conditions listed in the paragraph above. Also, new pianos are regulated with new parts such as many hundreds of small pieces of felt where even a tolerance-loss of a few thousandths of an inch can cause serious trouble in operation. Packing and settling of new felting causes much trouble in new pianos.

Investigate the competency of your service man very

thoroughly. If you blindly choose to have your piano work done solely on the basis of price, your piano probably will pass through the hands of an endless succession of tuning pirates, who will have absolutely no interest in maintaining the instrument as a whole. Each will leave the major repairing or regulating (the time-consuming jobs) to the next fellow. Your piano, your music, and your pocketbook will all suffer.

A wise piano owner will have his piano serviced regularly by the *same* qualified piano tuner-technician. A good technician will check for faults in the action regulating on each tuning visit. He can do much (through spot regulating) to keep the piano machinery operating at its best from year to year (at minor expense) and put off the day when the piano may require a complete regulating with new key felts, etc. This kind of preventive care pays dividends in piano life just as similar preventive techniques help to preserve your own life.

56. WHAT IS MEANT BY VOICING OR TONE-REGULATING A PIANO?

The term *tone-regulating* is technically correct for this procedure, but by virtue of popular usage *voicing* has come to mean practically the same thing. Many piano owners confuse action regulating (see Item 55) with tone-regulating. In order to avoid such misunderstanding, let us use the term *voicing* for this procedure.

Voicing can be defined as the delicate art of altering and leveling up tonal response throughout the entire range of the piano scale by adjusting the outer tension and inner compression of hammer-head felts. The intricacies of this operation may be better appreciated by observing that even among highly qualified piano technicians, an expert "voicer" is the exception rather than the rule. And among piano tuners in general he is something of a rarity.

The piano owner must realize that before a job of piano

hammer voicing is attempted, the subject piano must first be in acceptable mechanical repair and regulation; and it must be at the correct pitch and in perfect tune. If the piano has been neglected, this could mean additional work and expense before the piano is ready for voicing. It is surprising how many professional pianists, semiprofessionals, music directors, and teachers of piano music seem not to know this. The general idea seems to be that "voicing" is something entirely separate from the other needs of the piano.

Voicing is the final artistic touch to an otherwise perfectly conditioned instrument.

More often than not, a piano needs a good action regulating and fine tuning much more than it needs actual voicing. Some pianos, after undergoing this preconditioning, respond so well tonally that the need for a complete voicing job is unnecessary. A few hammer heads touched up here and there will then add the final perfection of tone.

If a piano owner is unwilling to have his instrument preconditioned, he should forget about having the instrument voiced. Under such conditions, any attempt at voicing is doomed to failure.

Piano hammer conditioning is tremendously important to the production of good tone. To preserve tone we must preserve the resiliency and quality of the hammer felt. While voicing alone may be required on piano hammers that are relatively new; older, worn piano hammers may require reshaping to correct contour and realignment with the strings (assuming that the old hammers are worth saving). When hammer felts are too badly worn, motheaten, or ruined by amateur attempts at self-service, there is no other alternative but to replace the set of hammer heads.

The quoted fee (an estimate) for voicing will not include such extra work as reshaping hammer felts, regluing loose hammer heads, and realigning hammers to strings. These operations are not necessary in every instance, so they are charged for separately. Prices quoted for voicing piano hammers may vary from a few dollars for touching up a few tinny or snarling notes to ten times as much for going over the entire set of hammers to produce a particular shade of tone throughout.

Never allow anyone but a qualified expert to voice the hammers of a high-quality piano. The amateur or other incompetent can ruin a fine set of expensive piano hammers in a matter of minutes. If there is the slightest doubt in your mind about a piano service man's ability to do the job right the first time, forego that voicing job. This is as important to the piano service man as it is to the piano owner. There are as many shades of hammer voicing and resultant shades of "tone color" as there are shades of blue. It is important that the "voicer" enjoy the complete confidence of the customer if he is to satisfy that customer's discriminating taste in piano tone. Neither the voicer nor the customer can afford to do business on any other footing.

Where several or more people use the same piano, no one shade of voicing will be equally appreciated by all. Tastes vary, and no two human beings hear exactly alike. In such instances, the voicer's only alternative is to adopt the policy and aim of factory voicing: a compromise tonality intended to please the average listener.

57. MOVING THE PIANO

Pianos are exceedingly heavy and awkward to handle. Piano moving is a task for professionals who are trained, well-equipped, insured, and fully aware of the risks involved in handling a valuable musical instrument. Consult the professional mover, rather than your friends or neighbors, about moving your piano. You may well avoid injury to yourself and others, and lawsuits, to say nothing of damage to the piano, doorways, stairs, walls, and carpeting.

Note: After a grand piano has been moved and set up again, the piano owner should double-check the reassembly of the lyre and especially the legs to make certain that all are in working order and well secured by lock plates, safety screws, or other means. (It might be advisable to check leg security under that old grand right now. It is a hair-raising experience to call at a home where small children crawl around under the grand piano and then to discover that the cast-iron leg plates are cracked and broken and safety screws are either loose or missing.)

58. SHOULD A PIANO BE TUNED AFTER IT IS MOVED?

This is a question much asked by piano owners. They seem to expect a one-word answer that will fit all circumstances. This is not possible.

Pianos that are old (or even new pianos that are cheaply assembled) may be structurally weak and go out of tune at the slightest excuse. You should move such pianos very cautiously if you wish them to retain tuning.

But let us assume that your piano is structurally sound, at proper pitch, and in tune at the time you decide to move it. Need for tuning your piano after it has been moved will depend on where, when, and how it was moved.

A. If a piano is moved from one part of the country to another, from one home to another, by any means whatever, it should be checked and tuned again, observing the three-to-six-weeks' acclimation period described in Item 24. Of course, if there is shipping damage (or suspected damage) the piano should be checked immediately. If damage is verified, you should notify the cartage company.

B. If a piano is moved from an upper floor to a basement, or vice versa, it should be tuned in from three to six weeks.

C. If a piano is moved from one room to another in your home (same floor) *it may or may not need tuning again because of the move*. It may be all right until your piano tuner's regular visit, providing you have the piano tuned as often as you should. Everything depends on how carefully you moved the piano plus differences of humidity, aridity, heat, or cold between the two locations. You will have to judge these things.

D. If a piano is moved from one location to another in the same room of your home, there can easily be a change in atmospheric conditions (drafts from doorways, direct sunlight from windows). Your answer will be found in "C" above.

E. If a piano located in a school is continually moved from one room to another, it should receive at least four tunings per school year and as many more tunings as are necessary to keep that particular piano in tune and at proper pitch. (Most school pianos take a terrific beating through misuse and neglect. Read Items 42 and 43.)

F. Special circumstances necessitate special measures whenever a piano is handled or moved. Proper care will never harm your piano.

59. PIANO LOCATION IN THE HOME

The location afforded the piano in the home will definitely have a bearing on tuning stability, mechanical operation, tone, and even the finish. A few important things to consider are listed below:

1. The ideal room temperature for a piano is 72 degrees Fahrenheit. Excessive variations in temperature should be avoided.

2. Relative humidity should be kept around 40 percent and as constant as possible. Too dry air (below 40 percent), or relative humidity ranging above 40 percent are hard on pianos as well as on humans. This is especially true for the piano where relative humidity seesaws back and forth between the two extremes (secure a humidity gauge).

There is only one exception to the 40-percent relative-humidity ideal. Player pianos and reproducers should be afforded a relative humidity of around 50 percent. This level of moisture in the air prevents drying out the "player" assembly and prevents leakage and loss of power. One must live with the fact that the relative humidity level of 50 percent is a bit high for the rest of the instrument.

3. If your home is well insulated, it is permissible to place the piano along an outside wall. But do allow a four- to six-inch air space between the piano back and the wall. This will keep a constant temperature on both sides of the soundboard and also prevent a muffled tone.

4. Locate pianos away from ducts that feed either hot or cold air into a room. This also applies to hot-water radiators and radiant-heat installations. Much piano damage is caused by carelessness in this respect.

5. Pianos should be kept out of direct drafts from any source.

6. Never place a piano under a window, even on the north wall (sometimes done to avoid direct sunlight). Windows are heat-cheaters, and creeping winter cold or condensed moisture on the glass will not help your piano.

7. Try to locate the piano away from the direct rays of the sun. Direct sunlight will cause the finest piano finish to deteriorate before its time. It also can have a devastating effect on tunings and various mechanical parts.

One often finds extreme conditions in regard to sun exposure in our schools. Almost invariably the school piano is backed up to the windows (away from the blackboards) where the rear of the soundboard is exposed to continuously varying degrees of coolness and hot sunlight. The result is to dry out the tuning-pin block, while the wooden soundboard endures a ceaseless cycle of expansion and contraction, thereby destroying tuning stability and eventually cracking up or warping and pulling loose from the ribs. This kind of treatment is an excellent way to send well-conceived, as well as low-quality, pianos to the scrap heap in a relatively short time.

8. Avoid positioning a piano under a ceiling duct for an air-conditioner or (in reference to a grand piano) over a floor duct used for the same purpose.

9. Remember that a room with many alcoves and much drapery and carpeting will tend to distort and deaden piano tone.

60. MOTH PREVENTION AND EXTERMINATION IN THE PIANO

While people are aware of the dangers of moth and carpet beetle damage to clothing, rugs, carpeting, and other woolens in the home, many piano owners remain unaware of the same dangers of infestation to the several thousand separate pieces of high-quality wool felt within the piano.

Moths, carpet beetles, and termites cause hundreds of thousands of dollars' worth of damage to pianos every year. Every part of the piano, including the felts, is vital to the overall performance of the instrument. We must do all in our power to protect the piano felts from infestation.

Possibly more than 50 percent of the pianos now in existence in the United States have at some time in their histories been subjected to the ravages of moths, carpet beetles, or termites.

Piano owners must not be lulled into a false security by current claims that the felts installed in new pianos today are permanently moth-proofed. *As of this writing, no sure-fire, permanent, piano-felt proofing against moths and carpet beetles has been discovered.* The felts installed in today's pianos are not permanently moth- or beetle-proofed. Such felting has been rendered *temporarily resistant* to these pests, which is something else entirely. The lethal qualities of the treated felting become ineffective with time (a few years at most) and then the felting is once more liable to infestation.

Pest control inside the piano presents problems that are unique. Unlike the proofing of felt destined for uses in other fields where experimentation has yielded various degrees of success, the need in pianos is for a permanent pest-proofing method that will not have detrimental effects on various other materials used in piano building such as wood, steel, iron, brass, copper, rubber, and plastics. This is a hard nut to crack.

(Note: All known moth and beetle insecticides available on the open market today are injurious to several or more piano materials and also could be dangerous to humans. Do not attempt to use them in your piano.)

Extensive research by the piano industry, felt manufacturers, several universities, and the United States Department of Agriculture offers hope that this problem will be solved. But until that day, it is advisable to employ time-tested methods of combating moths, carpet beetles, and other pests in pianos:

1. Keep insects out of the house or any other area that houses a piano.
2. Have your piano serviced regularly (at least twice a year) by a qualified piano service man. He will keep a weather eye out for inroads made by insect pests.
3. Have your piano service man give the inner workings of your piano thorough and periodic cleanings. A clean

piano is usually a safe piano. Temporary moth-proofing might also be applied at this time.

4. A small cloth bag or a paper dish containing a few old-fashioned mothballs is sometimes used in the bottom of vertical pianos to discourage moths. Another method is to deposit a small fistful of fresh, loose, very strong chewing tobacco inside the piano bottom, and a few ounces of the same material in the key frame cavities under the keys. Use of the latter and rather unorthodox method of pest control inside the piano is a local tuner's remedy from the distant past; but exceedingly effective— if you don't mind a slight odor of chewing tobacco. Not one of the pianos treated with the tobacco method showed any signs of damage from the usual pests, and extensive inquiries of the piano owners indicated rather conclusively that the unorthodox tobacco treatment had been initiated a half-century or more in the past.

Where neglect has allowed moths, carpet beetles, or termites to cause extensive damage to a piano, a complete job of extermination may be required, along with the major repairs, reconditioning, or rebuilding necessary to restore the instrument to use.

61. THAT PESKY MOUSE

Mice can be a real trial to piano owners, especially in rural areas when the crops are in and the weather turns cold. A seldom-used or neglected piano offers an ideal haven for these creatures. The inside of the piano is dark, and safe from prowling felines, with an abundance of nest-building materials nearby, including cloth, strong cord, leather, and an ample supply of nice felting. And there is plenty of wood to gnaw for exercise or to sharpen the teeth.

That pesky mouse, along with moths, carpet beetles, and

termites, is your enemy. Don't underestimate his destructive tendencies. In some areas he is responsible for more piano damage than are his listed allies. The wise piano owner will take all advisable means to guard against him:

1. Keep mice out of the house or any other area that houses a piano.
2. Have your piano serviced regularly (at least twice a year) by a qualified piano service man. Have him check out the instrument for signs of mice.
3. Periodic inspection and cleaning of inner workings is good insurance for your investment.

Don't expect protection from the family cat. He is usually too well-fed to be a threat to any mouse. And besides, Old Tom can't get around inside the piano.

Avoid the use of ordinary mouse poisons inside the piano. Arsenic and other chemicals contained in these preparations are damaging to piano felts, cloths, and other materials. It also could be dangerous to persons called in to service the instrument. Finally, the mother mouse and eight or ten youngsters might succumb in the family nest under the piano keys, and that could present another kind of problem.

62. HOW TO CLEAN
THE PIANO KEYS

Through the years manufacturers have used various materials for covering piano keys. These materials include genuine elephant ivory, walrus ivory, celluloids that resemble ivory, and modern white plastics; also lacquered ebony, substitute woods for ebony, and black plastics, to name a few. Each of these materials may react in a different manner when brought into contact with the same chemical cleaner or solvent. Unfavorable reactions could be disastrous.

The different key-covering materials have been glued and

cemented into place with a multitude of hot and cold adhesives of varying compositions. These adhesives will also react in unpredictable ways when brought into contact with a particular chemical cleaner or solvent (some coverings are porous). One type of glue will hold fast, while another will weaken. And who is to say exactly what kind of glue was used to fasten key coverings in a particular brand of piano made thirty or more years ago—or last week, for that matter?

The piano owner should refrain from using any kind of chemical agent to clean the keys of his piano.

The key coverings of thousands of older pianos, and some relatively new ones, have peeled off, warped, shrunk, or otherwise been ruined by failure to heed such advice.

Play it safe. A soft white cloth, *slightly dampened* with plain water (wrung almost dry) can be used to wipe off the black keys. Use a second piece of dampened cloth to clean the white key coverings. Avoid too much pressure, and do not snag the cloth on the protruding ends of the key tops.

Our purpose is to clean the coverings without allowing moisture to penetrate to the wood of the key underneath. Too much moisture on bare wood will cause the latter to swell and weaken the glue bond between wood and covering. It is better to use too little moisture on the cloth than to use too much. A drop or two of very gentle liquid soap may be added to the water if necessary, but use restraint. *Never* add anything else, including powdered abrasive cleansers, which will destroy the polish. When the keys are clean, polish them lightly with a soft, dry cloth.

Modern plastic key coverings are practically impervious to discoloration. But ivory will stain easily and discolor or yellow with age. The only satisfactory remedy for this condition is to have the piano service man remove the keys from the piano and take them to his shop for scraping, polishing, and general restoration; or to replace the faulty coverings with new.

63. THE PIANO FINISH
AND ITS CARE

The average piano owner might find it extremely difficult to determine exactly what type of wood finish was originally applied to his instrument. The outer coat or coats of finish could be one of any number of natural varnishes, synthetic varnishes, lacquers, wax-covered sealers, plastics, or other material; all of which vary within themselves in quality and content. There also is a great deal of variation in the *number* of applied coats of finishing materials. A low-cost piano might be finished with a bare minimum of low-cost materials, while a higher-priced instrument usually is finished with a greater number of coats of much finer finishing materials.

Owing to the great diversity of piano-finishing materials and methods of application, any attempt to set up concrete rules to be followed in the selection of cleaning and polishing agents for pianos in general would be extremely foolish and misleading.

However, the piano owner should avoid all polishing and cleaning agents containing silicon. This ingredient lends itself to a high polish, but should your piano ever need repairs to the finish or complete refinishing, the silicon absorbed by the finish through the years could interfere with the repairs.

Owners of new pianos have an advantage in that they have access to necessary information through current manufacturers. Some companies even furnish small containers of "touch-up" finishing materials to their customers (in matching colors) to be used on minor nicks and scratches. But the great majority of piano owners (with older instruments) will have to select their cleaning, polishing, and waxing materials themselves.

There are many good cleaning, polishing, and waxing compositions on the market. In general, any good-quality product that does not contain silicon and is offered to preserve the finish on fine furniture is acceptable for use on the piano case. Polishes containing lemon oil are favored by many piano owners. For further hints on preserving the piano finish, see Item 59.

64. THE QUOTED TUNING FEE, AND THE SERVICE IT INCLUDES

The tuning fee quoted by your piano tuner is the charge made to tune a regularly serviced piano into harmony. (See Items 43, 44, and 45.) It also is the charge made to tune a previously neglected piano into harmony, *after* completion of the separate jobs of making necessary regulations and repairs and establishing the correct overall piano pitch. The quoted tuning fee does *not* include any of the following services:

1. Extra work to correct overall pitch.
2. Repairs made necessary through breakage of faulty, worn, aged, rusted strings, or other parts.
3. Repairs or adjustments on pedals, trapwork, action, keys, case, casters, etc.
4. Work on loose tuning pins.
5. Traveling charges.
6. Piano appraisal.
7. Patching of piano finish.
8. Cleaning or vacuuming.
9. Moth prevention or extermination.
10. Other work.

It is only by keeping the work covered by the tuning fee within prescribed limits that a piano service man can operate successfully, maintain good customer relations, and protect himself against exploitation by those few people who would seek to gain advantage.

65. FEES FOR SERVICE CALLS, PIANO APPRAISALS, AND REPAIR ESTIMATES

In general, the following service practices hold true:

1. A *service-call* fee is charged by most reputable piano service people; but unlike similar fees in other service fields, *it is not an additional technical charge.* It is used when, owing to circumstances beyond the tuner's control, the visit results in no actual work performed, or work performed totals less than the minimum service-call fee.

2. A *piano-appraisal* fee usually pertains to a qualified, professional opinion regarding the condition and value of a used piano. Many people request this service with a view to either selling used pianos or buying them from private owners.

3. A *repair-estimate* fee is charged when the piano technician makes a requested repair estimate, but usually with the provision that should the recommended work be started immediately the cost of the estimate will be deducted from the total cost of the job. This fee, like the service-call fee, is primarily a protective business measure.

66. A SERVICE-FEE GUIDE

Publication of a piano-owner service-fee guide in a world of fast-changing prices is understandably a precarious affair. Piano service costs may vary with the time, place, and professional qualifications of the service man.

However, an attempt must be made to inform piano owners about various legitimate fees for qualified, competent, piano services. The following *guide* has been limited to the *basic estimated costs* (as of 1974) of only the most frequently encountered piano needs. The piano owner must remember that prices quoted for piano work by any source at any time are usually basically estimated costs and are not inflexible. He should consult his own local piano service man regarding actual costs for any item of work.

The following service-fee guide is based on top-quality, professional workmanship using the best materials. It is fairly representative of today's piano service costs.

1974
GENERAL SERVICES—BASIC CHARGES

NEW CUSTOMER   Basic fee (tuning only): 25.00–35.00

PIANOS RECEIVING REGULAR PERIODIC SERVICE
Tuned twice a year or more (Local) (each tuning): 20.00–25.00

COUNTRY & OUTSIDE AREA SERVICE
Tuning all styles: (see rates listed above)
Plus mileage (rate ____) (____) miles:
Plus travel time (rate ____) (____) hours:
Country Group Travel costs (shared expenses):
    When several customers within the same area receive service on the same trip.

CORRECTION OF PITCH (*overall balanced string tension*)
Raise pitch ¼ tone or less (additional): 15.00
Raise pitch ¼ to ½ tone (additional): 20.00
Raise pitch more than ½ tone (additional): 30.00
Lower pitch (additional): 15.00–20.00
    (American Standard Pitch is A-440 cps.)

SERVICE CALL
  Local: 10.00–15.00
  Outside (travel time & mileage additional): 10.00–15.00

SERVICE ESTIMATE OR PIANO APPRAISAL (*each piano*)
  Local: 20.00–25.00
  Outside (travel time & mileage additional): 20.00–25.00

CHURCH, SCHOOL, COMMERCIAL WORK
  (estimates only)

CLEANING
  Piano action and interior of piano: 20.00–30.00
  Grand-piano soundboard: cost determined on job

MOTH-PROOFING ALL FELTS (*temporary*) (*See Item 60, Part Four.*)
  Includes extermination and/or prevention: 40.00

COMPLETE ACTION REGULATING (*repairs are additional*)
  Grands (includes necessary
    regulating materials): 140.00–160.00
  Verticals (includes necessary
    regulating materials): 100.00–125.00
  Partial regulating: cost determined on job

RESHAPING WORN HAMMERS TO PROPER CONTOUR: 45.00

TONE REGULATING OF HAMMERS (*voicing*): 30.00

LOOSE TUNING PINS
  Driving tuning pins, setting string coils, etc.: 20.00–40.00
  Application of pin-block restorer fluids: 50.00–75.00

BRIDLE STRAPS
  New set (labor and material): 45.00
  Partial sets: cost determined on job

REMOVAL OF CERTAIN SPINET DROP ACTIONS: 6.00–10.00
  (For explanation see part B, Item 9, Part One.)

NEW STRINGS

New bass string (custom made) (labor and material): 12.00
New bass string (Universal) (labor and material): 10.00
Steel string (treble) (labor and material): 6.00–9.00
New bass strings (set—new pins) (labor and material): 150.00.
Complete restringing of piano (new tuning pins): 350.00–450.00
(Cartage at owner's expense.)

KEYS

Set of new plastic tops (all pianos) (includes labor, material, local pickup and delivery, key leveling, and adjusting): 85.00
Set of new plastic fronts (labor and material): 60.00
Set of new plastic sharps (labor and material): 50.00
Set of ebony sharps (labor and material): 65.00
Set of new key buttons (labor and material): 75.00
Key fronts and centers rebushed (labor and material) both: 80.00
Individual key repair: cost determined on job

MISCELLANEOUS WORK

Adjustments and repairs to rods, levers, pedals, casters, case parts, soundboard, bridges, old strings, etc.: cost determined on job

Costs of new sets of replacement items for all pianos will be furnished by qualified technicians on request. Quoted estimates should include cost of materials and labor.

REFINISHING OF PIANOS—*All styles:* 300.00–600.00

(Costs depend on type and condition of piano case and the type of finish desired [rubbed satin effect, high polish, closed or open pore finishes, bleached or special finishes, etc.]. Cartage at owner's expense.)

Special Attention: Always engage a qualified piano service man to take care of refinishing jobs. He knows how to safeguard *the instrument inside the case* while refinishing. There are far too many amateurs, quacks, and part-time finishing buffs who offer to refinish pianos and who are totally unaware of the special care necessary to refinishing a valuable *musical instrument.* In such hands, a fine piano can suffer permanent damage. It deserves better treatment, including the painstaking building up of an entirely new finish from the bare wood using an approved finishing schedule with the correct top-quality materials.

67. PIANO SERVICE AGREEMENTS

If it is at all possible for you to enter into a *piano service agreement* with a well-qualified, permanently established piano tuner-technician in or near your area, do so. It is by far the best way to take proper care of your piano. Such an agreement should call for a minimum of two tunings a year. If a tuner-technician agrees to less, he is merely giving "lip-service" to proper piano care. To fail to follow through in one's own service business (as some piano service people do) is to be equally as guilty of piano neglect as the piano owners who are parties to such arrangements.

68. THE PIANO TECHNICIANS GUILD, INC., SYMBOL OF QUALITY PIANO SERVICE

THE PIANO TECHNICIANS GUILD *is a non-profit organization of highly trained piano craftsmen, international in scope, with headquarters in the United States of America and Chapters in every State and Canada.*

Check the yellow pages of your phone book. There may be a Chapter in your immediate area. Requests for service information can be made to the home office or any Chapter.

The current address for the national headquarters is P. O. Box 1813, Seattle, Washington, 98111.

Index